GERMAN STORIES

FOR BEGINNERS

DIVE INTO GERMAN CULTURE, EXPAND YOUR VOCABULARY, AND MASTER BASICS THE FUN WAY!

BY ADRIAN GEE

ISBN: 979-8-322720-42-3

Author's Note

Welcome to "69 Short German Stories for Beginners"! It's my absolute pleasure to guide you through the fascinating journey of learning German, a language with a profound historical significance and immense cultural richness. This collection of stories is designed to open doors to an engaging and effective way of expanding your vocabulary, mastering basic grammatical structures, and developing a true love for the German language.

My passion for languages and education has led me to create this unique compilation, aiming to make German language learning accessible, enjoyable, and deeply rewarding for beginners. Each story is carefully crafted to not only provide linguistic insights but also to spark your imagination and curiosity, making language learning an adventure rather than a chore.

Connect with Me: Join our language learning community on Instagram: @adriangruszka. Share your German learning journey, and let's celebrate your progress together!

Sharing is Caring: If you find joy and progress in your German studies with this book, please share it and tag me on social media. Your feedback is invaluable, and I look forward to seeing how these stories enhance your learning.

Diving into "69 Short German Stories for Beginners" is more than learning a language; it's about discovering new perspectives and the beauty of German culture. Embrace the adventure and enjoy every step towards fluency. Viel Erfolg! (Good luck!)

- *Adrian Gee*

CONTENTS

INTRODUCTION

Welcome

Welcome to "69 Short German Stories for Beginners," your gateway to learning German through engaging and carefully crafted stories. Whether you're a complete beginner or someone looking to refresh their skills, this book offers a unique approach to mastering the basics of the German language. Let's embark on this linguistic adventure together!

What the Book is About

This book is designed with the beginner in mind, providing a diverse collection of 69 short stories that span various genres and themes. Each story is constructed to introduce you to basic German vocabulary, grammar structures, and cultural nuances in an enjoyable and digestible format. Unlike traditional textbooks, these stories are intended to captivate your interest and stimulate your learning process, making German more accessible and fun to learn.

How the Book is Laid Out

Each story is followed by a glossary of key terms used in the tale, helping you expand your vocabulary. Following the glossary, comprehension questions and a summary in German challenge you to use your new skills and ensure you've understood what you've read. This format is designed to reinforce the material, improve your reading comprehension, and encourage active learning.

Recommendations and Tips on How to Get the Most Out of the Book

1. **Read Regularly:** Consistency is key when learning a new language. Try to read at least one story per day to maintain progress and build your confidence in understanding German.

2. **Use the Glossary:** Refer to the glossary often to familiarize yourself with new words and phrases. Try to use them in your daily practice to enhance retention.

3. **Engage with the Comprehension Questions:** Answer the questions at the end of each story to test your understanding. This reinforces learning and boosts your ability to use German in context.

4. **Practice Out Loud:** Reading aloud helps with pronunciation and fluency. Read the stories or summaries aloud to get comfortable speaking German.

5. **Immerse Yourself:** Beyond this book, try to immerse yourself in the German language through music, movies, and conversation with native speakers. This real-world exposure complements your learning and deepens your cultural understanding.

- Chapter One -
THE LOST KEY

Der verlorene Schlüssel

Eines sonnigen Morgens kann Anna ihren Schlüssel nicht finden. Sie benötigt den Schlüssel, um ihre Haustür zu öffnen. Anna beginnt überall zu suchen.

Zuerst schaut sie in ihre Tasche. "Ist mein Schlüssel in meiner Tasche?" denkt sie. Doch die Tasche ist leer.

Dann erinnert sich Anna, dass sie den Schlüssel möglicherweise im Haus gelassen hat. Sie geht zum Fenster, um hineinzuschauen. Aber sie kann den Schlüssel nicht sehen.

Als Nächstes beschließt Anna, unter der Fußmatte zu suchen. Viele Leute verstecken dort einen Ersatzschlüssel. Sie hebt die Fußmatte hoch, aber der Schlüssel ist nicht da.

Anna beginnt traurig zu werden. Sie braucht Hilfe. Sie ruft ihren Freund Tom an. "Tom, ich habe meinen Schlüssel verloren. Kannst du mir beim Suchen helfen?" fragt sie.

Tom kommt schnell. Zusammen suchen sie hinter dem Blumentopf vor dem Haus. Und dort finden sie den Schlüssel!

"Danke, Tom! Du hast mir geholfen, meinen Schlüssel zu finden," sagt Anna glücklich. Jetzt kann sie die Tür öffnen und in ihr Haus gehen.

Vocabulary

Key	*Schlüssel*
Find	*Finden*
Door	*Tür*
Lost	*Verloren*
Search	*Suchen*
House	*Haus*
Open	*Öffnen*
Pocket	*Tasche*
Remember	*Erinnern*
Floor	*Boden*
Under	*Unter*
Behind	*Hinter*
Front	*Vorne*
Inside	*Innen*
Help	*Hilfe*

Questions About the Story

1. *What does Anna need to open?*

   a) Her car
   b) Her house door
   c) A window

2. *Where does Anna first look for her key?*

   a) Under the doormat
   b) In her pocket
   c) Behind the flowerpot

3. *What is Anna's reaction when her pocket is empty?*

   a) She is happy
   b) She is relieved
   c) She is sad

4. *Who does Anna call for help?*

   a) Her neighbor
   b) A locksmith
   c) Her friend, Tom

5. *Where was the key finally found?*

   a) Inside the house
   b) Under the doormat
   c) Behind the flowerpot

Correct Answers:

1. b) Her house door
2. b) In her pocket
3. c) She is sad
4. c) Her friend, Tom
5. c) Behind the flowerpot

- Chapter Two -
A DAY AT THE PARK

Ein Tag im Park

Lucy und ihr Freund Max beschließen, einen Tag im Park zu verbringen. Der Park ist voller hoher Bäume und der Himmel ist klar und blau. Sie bringen einen Ball zum Spielen und ein Picknick mit, um es unter den grünen Bäumen zu genießen.

Während sie zu ihrem Lieblingsplatz gehen, sehen sie Vögel über sich fliegen und Blumen in vielen Farben. Die Sonne scheint hell und macht den Tag perfekt für ein Picknick.

Sie breiten eine Decke auf dem Gras nahe einer Bank aus und richten ihr Picknick her. Nach dem Essen sagt Lucy: "Lass uns mit dem Ball spielen!" Sie rennen herum, werfen und fangen den Ball und lachen die ganze Zeit.

Nach dem Spielen setzen sie sich auf die Bank, schauen in den Himmel und ruhen sich aus. "Ich liebe solche Tage," sagt Max lächelnd. Lucy nickt: "Ich auch, es ist so friedlich hier."

Als die Sonne zu sinken beginnt, packen sie zusammen und gehen nach Hause, glücklich nach einem wunderbaren Tag im Park.

Vocabulary

Park	*Park*
Tree	*Baum*
Play	*Spielen*
Ball	*Ball*
Run	*Rennen*
Friend	*Freund*
Laugh	*Lachen*
Bench	*Bank*
Bird	*Vogel*
Sky	*Himmel*
Green	*Grün*
Flower	*Blume*
Sun	*Sonne*
Picnic	*Picknick*
Walk	*Gehen*

Questions About the Story

1. *Who did Lucy go to the park with?*

    a) Her dog
    b) Her brother
    c) Her friend, Max

2. *What did Lucy and Max bring to the park?*

    a) A kite
    b) A ball and a picnic
    c) Bicycles

3. *What color was the sky when Lucy and Max went to the park?*

    a) Grey and cloudy
    b) Clear and blue
    c) Rainy and dark

4. *What did they see as they walked to their favorite spot?*

    a) Cats running around
    b) Ducks swimming in a pond
    c) Birds flying above and flowers of many colors

5. *What did they do after eating their picnic?*

    a) They went for a swim
    b) They took a nap
    c) They played with the ball

Correct Answers:

1. c) Her friend, Max
2. b) A ball and a picnic
3. b) Clear and blue
4. c) Birds flying above and flowers of many colors
5. c) They played with the ball

- Chapter Three -
BIRTHDAY SURPRISE

Geburtstagsüberraschung

Heute ist Mias Geburtstag, und ihre Freunde haben eine Überraschungsparty für sie geplant. Sie haben einen Kuchen, Luftballons und Dekorationen vorbereitet. Mia hat keine Ahnung von der Party.

Als Mia den Raum betritt, springen alle heraus und rufen: "Überraschung!" Mia ist schockiert, aber sehr glücklich. Sie sieht den Kuchen mit Kerzen und lächelt.

Ihre Freunde singen "Happy Birthday", und Mia bläst die Kerzen aus und macht einen Wunsch. Dann geben sie ihr Geschenke und Karten, um ihre Liebe und Wünsche für sie auszudrücken.

Der Raum ist erfüllt von Lachen und Freude, während sie feiern. Mia dankt allen: "Das ist die beste Geburtstagsüberraschung, die ich je hatte!"

Sie verbringen den Abend damit, Kuchen zu essen, Spiele zu spielen und die Party zu genießen. Mia fühlt sich dankbar, solch wunderbare Freunde zu haben.

Vocabulary

Birthday	Geburtstag
Cake	Kuchen
Party	Party
Gift	Geschenk
Surprise	Überraschung
Balloon	Luftballon
Invite	Einladen
Happy	Glücklich
Candle	Kerze
Sing	Singen
Friend	Freund
Card	Karte
Wish	Wunsch
Celebrate	Feiern
Decoration	Dekoration

Questions About the Story

1. *What occasion is being celebrated in the story?*

   a) A wedding
   b) An anniversary
   c) A birthday

2. *What do Mia's friends have ready for her?*

   a) A movie
   b) A concert ticket
   c) A cake, balloons, and decorations

3. *How does Mia react when her friends surprise her?*

   a) She is confused
   b) She is unhappy
   c) She is shocked but happy

4. *What do Mia's friends do after yelling "Surprise!"?*

   a) They leave the room
   b) They sing "Happy Birthday"
   c) They start dancing

5. *What does Mia do after her friends sing to her?*

   a) She leaves the party
   b) She cuts the cake
   c) She blows out the candles

Correct Answers:

1. c) A birthday
2. c) A cake, balloons, and decorations
3. c) She is shocked but happy
4. b) They sing "Happy Birthday"
5. c) She blows out the candles

- Chapter Four -
THE NEW NEIGHBOR

Die neue Nachbarin

Emily ist gerade in eine neue Wohnung in der Ahornstraße eingezogen. Sie ist nervös, aber aufgeregt, ihre Nachbarn kennenzulernen.

Während sie Kisten aus ihrem LKW auslädt, bemerkt sie, wie sich jemand nähert. Es ist ihr Nachbar von nebenan, Alex, der sie mit einem warmen Lächeln begrüßt.

"Hallo! Ich bin Alex. Ich wohne nebenan. Wenn du Hilfe brauchst, sag einfach Bescheid," sagt Alex und bietet ihre Hand an.

Emily ist dankbar und antwortet: "Danke, Alex! Vielleicht brauche ich später etwas Hilfe." Sie unterhalten sich eine Weile, und Alex bietet an, Emily anderen Nachbarn vorzustellen.

Später am Tag kommt Alex zurück und hilft Emily mit ihren Kisten. Dann machen sie einen Spaziergang durch die Straße, treffen andere freundliche Nachbarn, die Emily herzlich begrüßen.

Emily fühlt sich willkommen und glücklich, in die Ahornstraße gezogen zu sein und freut sich darauf, neue Freunde zu machen.

Vocabulary

Neighbor	*Nachbar*
Move	*Umziehen*
Welcome	*Begrüßen*
Apartment	*Wohnung*
Box	*Kiste*
New	*Neu*
Meet	*Treffen*
Help	*Helfen*
Introduce	*Vorstellen*
Friendly	*Freundlich*
Street	*Straße*
Next	*Nächster*
Doorbell	*Klingel*
Smile	*Lächeln*
Greet	*Begrüßen*

Questions About the Story

1. *How does Emily feel about meeting her new neighbors?*

   a) Indifferent
   b) Nervous but excited
   c) Scared

2. *Who approaches Emily as she is unloading her truck?*

   a) A delivery person
   b) A distant relative
   c) Her next-door neighbor, Alex

3. *What does Alex offer Emily?*

   a) A welcome gift
   b) To call for more help
   c) Help with her boxes

4. *What does Alex do later that day?*

   a) Invites Emily for dinner
   b) Comes back and helps with boxes
   c) Takes Emily to a party

5. *During their walk, what do Emily and Alex do?*

   a) Meet other friendly neighbors
   b) Go shopping
   c) Visit the local library

Correct Answers:

1. b) Nervous but excited
2. c) Her next-door neighbor, Alex
3. c) Help with her boxes
4. b) Comes back and helps with boxes
5. a) Meet other friendly neighbors

- Chapter Five -
LOST IN THE CITY

Verloren in der Stadt

Eines Tages fand sich Emma in der großen Stadt verloren. Sie hatte eine Karte, aber die Straßen verwirrten sie. "Wo bin ich?" fragte sie sich und schaute auf die Karte.

Zuerst versuchte sie, nach dem Weg zu fragen. Sie sprach eine freundlich aussehende Person an und fragte: "Entschuldigung, können Sie mir sagen, wie ich zur Hauptstraße komme?" Die Person wies sie zur Ecke.

Emma ging zur Ecke, aber die Ampeln und die belebten Gehwege ließen sie zögern. Sie musste die Straße überqueren, war sich aber nicht sicher, wann.

Sie fand einen Platz mit einem großen Schild, auf dem "Zentralbahnhof" stand. "Dahin muss ich zurück, um meinen Zug zu erreichen," erinnerte sich Emma.

Schließlich fand sie nach weiteren Nachfragen und Befolgung der Wegweisungen ihren Weg zurück zum Bahnhof. Sie war erleichtert und glücklich, ihren Weg gefunden zu haben. Von nun an versprach sie, mehr auf die Schilder zu achten und mehr über die Navigation in der Stadt zu lernen.

Vocabulary

City	Stadt
Map	Karte
Street	Straße
Lost	Verloren
Ask	Fragen
Direction	Richtung
Corner	Ecke
Traffic light	Ampel
Cross	Überqueren
Busy	Belebt
Find	Finden
Square	Platz
Sign	Schild
Return	Zurückkehren
Station	Bahnhof

Questions About the Story

1. *What did Emma have to help her find her way in the city?*

   a) A compass
   b) A map
   c) A guidebook

2. *Who did Emma first ask for directions?*

   a) A police officer
   b) A shopkeeper
   c) A friendly-looking person

3. *What made Emma hesitate while trying to navigate the city?*

   a) Rain
   b) The traffic lights and busy sidewalks
   c) Getting a phone call

4. *Where did Emma need to return to catch her train?*

   a) Main Street
   b) The airport
   c) Central Station

5. *How did Emma finally find her way back?*

   a) By using a GPS
   b) By following the signs
   c) By asking more people for directions

Correct Answers:

1. b) A map
2. c) A friendly-looking person
3. b) The traffic lights and busy sidewalks
4. c) Central Station
5. c) By asking more people for directions

- Chapter Six -
A PICNIC BY THE LAKE

Ein Picknick am See

Lucas und Mia beschlossen, an einem sonnigen Tag ein Picknick am See zu machen. Sie packten einen Korb mit Sandwiches, Obst und Getränken. Sie nahmen auch eine große Decke zum Sitzen und einige Spiele zum Spielen mit.

Als sie am See ankamen, breiteten sie die Decke auf dem Gras unter einem großen Baum aus. Der See sah unter der Sonne wunderschön aus, und Vögel flogen über ihre Köpfe.

Nachdem sie ihre Sandwiches gegessen und das Obst genossen hatten, sagte Lucas: "Lass uns mit dem Ball spielen!" Sie verbrachten einige Zeit mit Spielen und beschlossen dann, im See zu schwimmen.

Das Wasser war erfrischend, und sie hatten Spaß beim Schwimmen und Planschen. Nach dem Schwimmen legten sie sich auf die Decke, um sich zu entspannen und den Himmel zu beobachten.

"Es ist so friedlich hier," sagte Mia und lauschte den Vögeln und spürte die sanfte Sonne. Sie blieben bis zum Sonnenuntergang und genossen ihren perfekten Tag am See.

Vocabulary

Lake	*See*
Picnic	*Picknick*
Basket	*Korb*
Blanket	*Decke*
Sandwich	*Sandwich*
Fruit	*Obst*
Drink	*Getränk*
Friend	*Freund*
Sun	*Sonne*
Play	*Spielen*
Swim	*Schwimmen*
Tree	*Baum*
Grass	*Gras*
Relax	*Entspannen*
Bird	*Vogel*

Questions About the Story

1. *What did Lucas and Mia decide to do on a sunny day?*

    a) Go for a swim
    b) Have a picnic by the lake
    c) Play soccer

2. *What did they pack in their picnic basket?*

    a) Sandwiches, fruits, and drinks
    b) Pizza
    c) Burgers and fries

3. *Where did they spread the blanket for the picnic?*

    a) On the beach
    b) In a clearing
    c) Under a big tree

4. *What activity did Lucas suggest after eating?*

    a) Going home
    b) Swimming in the lake
    c) Playing with the ball

5. *How did they find the water when they went swimming?*

    a) Cold
    b) Too hot
    c) Refreshing

Correct Answers:

1. b) Have a picnic by the lake
2. a) Sandwiches, fruits, and drinks
3. c) Under a big tree
4. c) Playing with the ball
5. c) Refreshing

- Chapter Seven -
THE SCHOOL PROJECT

Das Schulprojekt

In Herrn Smiths Klasse wurde den Schülern ein Schulprojekt zugewiesen. Sie mussten in Teams arbeiten, um ein Thema zu recherchieren und dann der Klasse zu präsentieren.

Anna, Ben, Charlie und Dana bildeten ein Team. Sie beschlossen, die Bedeutung des Recyclings zu erforschen. Sie sammelten Informationen, erstellten einen Bericht und arbeiteten an einer Präsentation.

Am Tag der Präsentation waren sie nervös, aber bereit. Anna begann mit der Erklärung des Forschungsprozesses. Ben diskutierte die Vorteile des Recyclings und Charlie zeigte einige Statistiken. Dana schloss mit Ideen ab, wie man zu Hause und in der Schule mehr recyceln könnte.

Der Lehrer und die Klasse waren beeindruckt. Sie lernten viel und diskutierten, wie sie zu den Recyclingbemühungen beitragen könnten. Das Team war stolz auf seine Arbeit und glücklich, das Projekt erfolgreich abgeschlossen zu haben.

Vocabulary

Project	*Projekt*
School	*Schule*
Team	*Team*
Research	*Forschung*
Present	*Präsentieren*
Teacher	*Lehrer*
Class	*Klasse*
Learn	*Lernen*
Work	*Arbeiten*
Discuss	*Diskutieren*
Idea	*Idee*
Report	*Bericht*
Create	*Erstellen*
Group	*Gruppe*
Finish	*Beenden*

Questions About the Story

1. *What was the topic of the school project?*

   a) Global warming
   b) The importance of recycling
   c) Space exploration

2. *Who were the members of the team?*

   a) Anna, Ben, Charlie, and Dana
   b) Emily, Fred, George, and Hannah
   c) Isaac, Julia, Kyle, and Laura

3. *What did Ben discuss in the presentation?*

   a) The benefits of recycling
   b) How to plant a garden
   c) The process of photosynthesis

4. *What did the team create for their project?*

   a) A short film
   b) A magazine article
   c) A report and a presentation

5. *How did the team feel about their project?*

   a) Disappointed
   b) Confused
   c) Proud and happy

Correct Answers:

1. b) The importance of recycling
2. a) Anna, Ben, Charlie, and Dana
3. a) The benefits of recycling
4. c) A report and a presentation
5. c) Proud and happy

- Chapter Eight -
A WINTER'S TALE

Eine Winternachtgeschichte

An einem kalten Wintertag beschlossen Lily und Sam, den Schnee zu genießen. Sie zogen ihre Mäntel, Schals und Handschuhe an, um warm zu bleiben. Draußen war der Boden mit Schnee bedeckt und der Wind wehte sanft.

"Lass uns einen Schneemann bauen," schlug Lily vor. Gemeinsam rollten sie große Schneebälle für den Körper des Schneemanns und fanden Steine für seine Augen und den Mund. Sie lachten, als sie eine Karotte für die Nase platzierten.

Nachdem sie den Schneemann gebaut hatten, wurde ihnen sehr kalt. "Ich brauche etwas, um mich aufzuwärmen," sagte Sam. Also gingen sie hinein und machten heiße Schokolade. Das warme Getränk und der gemütliche Kamin ließen sie sich besser fühlen.

Später beschlossen sie, Skifahren zu probieren. Sie rutschten vorsichtig einen kleinen Hügel hinunter und spürten den kalten Wind. Skifahren machte Spaß, ließ sie aber wieder frieren.

Am Ende des Tages saßen sie am Kamin, fühlten die Wärme. "Das war der beste Wintertag," sagte Sam und Lily stimmte zu. Sie genossen die Schönheit des Winters aus der Wärme ihres Hauses.

Vocabulary

Winter	*Winter*
Snow	*Schnee*
Cold	*Kalt*
Coat	*Mantel*
Ice	*Eis*
Hot chocolate	*Heiße Schokolade*
Scarf	*Schal*
Ski	*Ski*
Snowman	*Schneemann*
Freeze	*Frieren*
Glove	*Handschuh*
Wind	*Wind*
Slide	*Rutschen*
Warm	*Warm*
Fireplace	*Kamin*

Questions About the Story

1. *What did Lily and Sam decide to do on a cold winter day?*

    a) Build a snowman
    b) Go skiing
    c) Make hot chocolate
    d) All of the above

2. *What did Lily suggest they make outside?*

    a) A snow angel
    b) A snowman
    c) An igloo

3. *What did they use for the snowman's nose?*

    a) A stone
    b) A stick
    c) A carrot

4. *What did Sam and Lily do to warm up after building the snowman?*

    a) Went for a walk
    b) Made hot chocolate
    c) Took a nap

5. *What activity did they try after warming up?*

    a) Ice skating
    b) Snowball fight
    c) Skiing

Correct Answers:

1. d) All of the above
2. b) A snowman
3. c) A carrot
4. b) Made hot chocolate
5. c) Skiing

- Chapter Nine -
THE MAGIC GARDEN

Der Zaubergarten

Lena entdeckte einen verborgenen Garten hinter dem Haus ihrer Großmutter, überwachsen und vergessen. Mit Neugier und Begeisterung beschloss sie, ihn wieder zum Leben zu erwecken.

Als Lena das Unkraut beseitigte und neue Samen pflanzte, bemerkte sie etwas Außergewöhnliches. Die Pflanzen wuchsen über Nacht, Blumen blühten sofort auf, und bisher ungesehene Schmetterlings- und Vogelarten begannen, den Garten zu besuchen.

Eines Tages fand Lena einen geheimnisvollen, alten Samen in einer Ecke des Gartens vergraben. Sie pflanzte ihn, und am nächsten Morgen war ein prächtiger Baum gewachsen, dessen Blätter in magischen Farben schimmerten.

Der Garten wurde zu Lenas Zuflucht, einem Ort, an dem Magie real war. Sie erfuhr, dass der Garten verzaubert war, gedeihend durch Pflege und Liebe. Hier konnte Lena mit den Pflanzen sprechen, und es schien, als würden sie zuhören, stärker und lebendiger wachsen.

Der Zaubergarten war nicht nur schön; er war lebendig, gefüllt mit Wundern und Geheimnissen, die darauf warteten, entdeckt zu werden. Lena wusste, dass sie die Hüterin dieses magischen Ortes war, ein verborgenes Juwel, wo die Grenze zwischen Realität und Magie verschwamm.

Vocabulary

Garden	*Garten*
Flower	*Blume*
Magic	*Magie*
Tree	*Baum*
Grow	*Wachsen*
Plant	*Pflanze*
Butterfly	*Schmetterling*
Bird	*Vogel*
Color	*Farbe*
Water	*Wasser*
Sunlight	*Sonnenlicht*
Seed	*Samen*
Leaf	*Blatt*
Beautiful	*Schön*
Nature	*Natur*

Questions About the Story

1. *What did Lena discover behind her grandmother's house?*

    a) A hidden garden
    b) A treasure chest
    c) An ancient book

2. *What extraordinary thing happened when Lena planted new seeds?*

    a) The seeds turned to gold
    b) The plants grew overnight
    c) The seeds sang songs

3. *What did Lena find buried in the garden?*

    a) A mysterious, ancient seed
    b) A map
    c) A magic wand

4. *What grew from the mysterious seed Lena planted?*

    a) A beanstalk
    b) A rose bush
    c) A magical tree

5. *What became Lena's sanctuary?*

    a) The forest
    b) The magic garden
    c) Her grandmother's house

Correct Answers:

1. a) A hidden garden
2. b) The plants grew overnight
3. a) A mysterious, ancient seed
4. c) A magical tree
5. b) The magic garden

- Chapter Ten -
A TRIP TO THE ZOO

Ein Ausflug in den Zoo

Jack und Emily beschlossen, ihren Samstag damit zu verbringen, den Stadtzoo zu erkunden, gespannt darauf, die vielfältige Tierwelt aus aller Welt zu sehen.

Ihre erste Station war das Löwengehege, wo sie die majestätischen Tiere beim Sonnenbaden beobachteten. Danach besuchten sie die Elefanten, fasziniert von deren sanfter Natur und Intelligenz.

Am Affengehege lachten Jack und Emily über die verspielten Streiche der Primaten, die von Ast zu Ast schwangen. Sie waren erstaunt über die Vielfalt der Arten und deren Verhalten.

Der Höhepunkt ihres Besuchs war die Fütterungszeit-Show, wo sie über die Ernährung und Pflege der Tiere lernten. Besonders beeindruckt waren sie von der Anmut der Giraffen und der Kraft der Bären.

Mit einem Zooplan in der Hand sorgten sie dafür, keine Ausstellung zu verpassen, von den tropischen Vögeln bis zum Reptilienhaus. Sie beendeten ihren Besuch mit einem Gespräch des Tierpflegers, der Einblicke in die Naturschutzbemühungen und die Bedeutung des Schutzes der Tierwelt gab.

Als sie den Zoo verließen, fühlten Jack und Emily ein erneuertes Staunen und eine tiefere Wertschätzung für die natürliche Welt. Sie versprachen zurückzukehren, begierig darauf, mehr zu lernen und ihr Abenteuer fortzusetzen.

Vocabulary

Zoo	*Zoo*
Animal	*Tier*
Lion	*Löwe*
Elephant	*Elefant*
Monkey	*Affe*
Cage	*Käfig*
Feed	*Füttern*
Visit	*Besuch*
Bear	*Bär*
Giraffe	*Giraffe*
Ticket	*Ticket*
Guide	*Führer*
Map	*Plan*
Show	*Show*
Learn	*Lernen*

Questions About the Story

1. *What was the first animal enclosure that Jack and Emily visited at the zoo?*

    a) Lions
    b) Elephants
    c) Monkeys

2. *What fascinated Jack and Emily about the elephants?*

    a) Their playful antics
    b) Their gentle nature and intelligence
    c) Their loud roars

3. *What did Jack and Emily find amusing at the monkey exhibit?*

    a) The monkeys sleeping
    b) The monkeys swinging from branch to branch
    c) The monkeys hiding

4. *What was the highlight of Jack and Emily's visit to the zoo?*

    a) The lion's roar
    b) The feeding time show
    c) The elephant ride

5. *Which animal's grace impressed Jack and Emily during the feeding time show?*

    a) Bears
    b) Monkeys
    c) Giraffes

Correct Answers:

1. a) Lions
2. b) Their gentle nature and intelligence
3. b) The monkeys swinging from branch to branch
4. b) The feeding time show
5. c) Giraffes

- Chapter Eleven -
COOKING CLASS

Kochkurs

Sarah entschied sich, einen Kochkurs zu besuchen, um neue Rezepte zu lernen. Der Kurs fand in einer großen Küche statt, auf dem Tisch waren viele Zutaten bereitgestellt.

Der Koch zeigte ihnen, wie man Zutaten mischt, um einen Kuchen zu machen. „Kochen ist wie Zauberei", sagte er, „mit dem richtigen Rezept kannst du etwas Köstliches kreieren."

Sarah folgte sorgfältig dem Rezept. Sie mischte, backte und kostete ihren Kuchen. Er war köstlich! Sie fühlte sich stolz und glücklich.

Sie lernte, Gemüse zu schneiden, Eier zu braten und Wasser für Pasta zu kochen. Jedes Gericht, das sie zubereitete, war ein neues Abenteuer.

Am Ende des Kurses genossen Sarah und ihre Klassenkameraden das gemeinsam gekochte Essen. Sie konnte es kaum erwarten, diese Gerichte zu Hause zu kochen.

Vocabulary

Cook	Kochen
Recipe	Rezept
Ingredient	Zutat
Kitchen	Küche
Oven	Ofen
Mix	Mischen
Bake	Backen
Taste	Kosten
Meal	Mahlzeit
Chef	Koch
Cut	Schneiden
Dish	Gericht
Spoon	Löffel
Fry	Braten
Boil	Kochen

Questions About the Story

1. *What did Sarah decide to join?*

   a) A dance class
   b) A cooking class
   c) A painting class

2. *What was the chef's analogy for cooking?*

   a) Cooking is like painting
   b) Cooking is like magic
   c) Cooking is like gardening

3. *What did Sarah feel after tasting her cake?*

   a) Disappointed
   b) Proud and happy
   c) Confused

4. *Which of the following skills did Sarah learn in the class?*

   a) Cutting vegetables
   b) Flying a kite
   c) Playing the guitar

5. *What did Sarah and her classmates do at the end of the class?*

   a) They went home immediately
   b) They cleaned the kitchen
   c) They enjoyed the meal they cooked

Correct Answers:

1. b) A cooking class
2. b) Cooking is like magic
3. b) Proud and happy
4. a) Cutting vegetables
5. c) They enjoyed the meal they cooked

- Chapter Twelve -
THE TREASURE HUNT

Die Schatzsuche

Tom und seine Freunde fanden eine alte Karte in einem Buch in der Bibliothek. Sie zeigte einen Schatz, der auf einer kleinen Insel versteckt war. Sie beschlossen, ein Abenteuer zu beginnen, um ihn zu finden.

Mit der Karte in der Hand suchten sie nach Hinweisen. Jeder Hinweis brachte sie dem Schatz näher. Sie mussten graben, den X-Markierungen folgen und Rätsel lösen.

Nach langer Suche entdeckten sie eine Truhe voller Gold! Sie konnten ihren Augen kaum trauen. Es war das Abenteuer ihres Lebens.

Sie beschlossen, das Gold mit ihrem Team zu teilen und einen Teil an die Bibliothek zu spenden. Ihre Schatzsuche war ein Erfolg, und sie lernten den Wert der Zusammenarbeit.

Vocabulary

Treasure	*Schatz*
Map	*Karte*
Search	*Suche*
Find	*Finden*
Clue	*Hinweis*
Dig	*Graben*
Island	*Insel*
Adventure	*Abenteuer*
Chest	*Truhe*
Gold	*Gold*
Mystery	*Geheimnis*
Team	*Team*
Follow	*Folgen*
X (marks the spot)	*X*
Discover	*Entdecken*

Questions About the Story

1. *Where did Tom and his friends find the old map?*

    a) In a book at the library
    b) In Tom's attic
    c) On the internet

2. *What did the map show?*

    a) A hidden cave
    b) A treasure on a small island
    c) A secret passage

3. *What did Tom and his friends have to do to find the treasure?*

    a) Ask for directions
    b) Solve mysteries
    c) Buy a new map

4. *What did they find at the end of their search?*

    a) A chest full of gold
    b) A new friend
    c) A lost puppy

5. *What did they decide to do with the gold?*

    a) Keep it all for themselves
    b) Throw it back into the sea
    c) Share it with their team and donate some to the library

Correct Answers:

1. a) In a book at the library
2. b) A treasure on a small island
3. b) Solve mysteries
4. a) A chest full of gold
5. c) Share it with their team and donate some to the library

- Chapter Thirteen -
A RAINY DAY

Ein regnerischer Tag

Es war ein regnerischer Tag, und Emily war in ihrem Haus gefangen. Sie beobachtete, wie die Regentropfen am Fenster herunterglitten und lauschte dem Donner.

Sie öffnete ihren Regenschirm und beschloss, draußen in Pfützen zu springen. Der Regen ließ alles frisch und neu aussehen.

Nass werdend, lachte sie und planschte im Wasser. Es machte Spaß, im Regen zu spielen und zu spüren, wie der Regenmantel sie davor schützte, zu nass zu werden.

Wieder drinnen fühlte sich Emily gemütlich. Sie machte sich ein heißes Getränk und setzte sich ans Fenster, um ihr Lieblingsbuch zu lesen.

Der regnerische Tag verwandelte sich für Emily in eine friedliche Zeit. Sie genoss das einfache Vergnügen, zu lesen und dem Regen zuzuschauen.

Vocabulary

Rain	Regen
Umbrella	Regenschirm
Puddle	Pfütze
Wet	Nass
Cloud	Wolke
Raincoat	Regenmantel
Drop	Tropfen
Splash	Planschen
Inside	Drinnen
Window	Fenster
Play	Spielen
Thunder	Donner
Lightning	Blitz
Cozy	Gemütlich
Read	Lesen

Questions About the Story

1. *What was Emily doing at the beginning of the story?*

    a) Reading a book
    b) Watching raindrops on the window
    c) Jumping in puddles

2. *What did Emily decide to do despite the rain?*

    a) Stay indoors and watch TV
    b) Go back to bed
    c) Jump in puddles outside

3. *What protected Emily from getting too wet?*

    a) Her raincoat
    b) A large tree
    c) An umbrella

4. *How did Emily feel playing in the rain?*

    a) Scared
    b) Excited
    c) Happy

5. *What did Emily do after coming back inside?*

    a) Took a nap
    b) Watched a movie
    c) Made herself a hot drink and read a book

Correct Answers:

1. b) Watching raindrops on the window
2. c) Jump in puddles outside
3. a) Her raincoat
4. c) Happy
5. c) Made herself a hot drink and read a book

- Chapter Fourteen -
AT THE SUPERMARKET

Im Supermarkt

Mike ging mit einer Liste in den Supermarkt. Er musste Lebensmittel für die Woche kaufen. Er schob den Einkaufswagen durch die Gänge und suchte nach Gemüse, Obst, Milch, Brot und Käse.

Er prüfte die Preise und legte die Artikel in seinen Wagen. Der Supermarkt war voll, aber Mike fand alles auf seiner Liste.

Als er mit dem Einkaufen fertig war, ging er zur Kasse, um zu bezahlen. Es gab einen Sonderverkauf auf Käse, daher sparte er etwas Geld. Darüber war Mike glücklich.

Nach dem Bezahlen verstaute er seine Einkäufe in Taschen und brachte sie zu seinem Auto. Er fühlte sich gut, weil er gesunde Lebensmittel für seine Familie gekauft hatte.

Vocabulary

Supermarket	Supermarkt
Cart	Einkaufswagen
Buy	Kaufen
Food	Lebensmittel
Price	Preis
Cashier	Kasse
List	Liste
Vegetable	Gemüse
Fruit	Obst
Milk	Milch
Bread	Brot
Cheese	Käse
Pay	Bezahlen
Sale	Verkauf
Bag	Tasche

Questions About the Story

1. *What was the main reason Mike went to the supermarket?*

    a) To buy clothes
    b) To buy food for the week
    c) To meet a friend

2. *Which of these items was NOT on Mike's shopping list?*

    a) Vegetables
    b) Fish
    c) Milk

3. *What did Mike do before putting items in his cart?*

    a) Checked the prices
    b) Called his friend
    c) Ate a snack

4. *Why was Mike happy after shopping?*

    a) He found a new job
    b) There was a sale on cheese
    c) He met a friend

5. *What did Mike do after finishing his shopping?*

    a) Went home directly
    b) Went to the cashier to pay
    c) Started shopping again

Correct Answers:

1. b) To buy food for the week
2. b) Fish
3. a) Checked the prices
4. b) There was a sale on cheese
5. b) Went to the cashier to pay

- Chapter Fifteen -
THE MUSIC LESSON

Die Musikstunde

Anna liebte Musik und beschloss, Musikunterricht zu nehmen. Sie wollte lernen, ein Instrument zu spielen.

Ihr Lehrer war Herr Smith. Er konnte Klavier und Gitarre spielen. Er war freundlich und geduldig.

In ihrer ersten Stunde lernte Anna, einfache Noten auf dem Klavier zu spielen. Sie versuchte sich auch im Singen eines Liedes. Es machte Spaß!

Herr Smith zeigte ihr, wie man Noten liest und den Rhythmus findet. Anna übte jeden Tag. Sie träumte davon, eines Tages in einer Band zu spielen.

Musik machte Anna glücklich. Sie freute sich darauf, mehr zu lernen und ihre Fähigkeiten zu verbessern.

Vocabulary

Music	Musik
Instrument	Instrument
Play	Spielen
Lesson	Unterricht
Teacher	Lehrer
Piano	Klavier
Guitar	Gitarre
Sing	Singen
Note	Note
Song	Lied
Practice	Üben
Band	Band
Sound	Klang
Rhythm	Rhythmus
Learn	Lernen

Questions About the Story

1. *What did Anna decide to take up?*

    a) Dance lessons
    b) Music lessons
    c) Art classes

2. *What instruments could Mr. Smith play?*

    a) Violin and drums
    b) Piano and guitar
    c) Flute and trumpet

3. *What did Anna learn in her first lesson?*

    a) How to dance
    b) How to play simple notes on the piano
    c) How to paint

4. *Besides playing the piano, what else did Anna try in her lesson?*

    a) Singing a song
    b) Playing the drums
    c) Drawing

5. *What did Mr. Smith teach Anna besides playing notes?*

    a) How to read music notes and find the rhythm
    b) How to write her own music
    c) How to conduct an orchestra

Correct Answers:

1. b) Music lessons
2. b) Piano and guitar
3. b) How to play simple notes on the piano
4. a) Singing a song
5. a) How to read music notes and find the rhythm

- Chapter Sixteen -
THE LOST PUPPY

Der verlorene Welpe

Lucy fand einen verlorenen Welpen auf der Straße. Der Welpe hatte kein Halsband, war aber sehr freundlich und zutraulich.

Sie beschloss, nach dem Besitzer des Welpen zu suchen. Sie erstellte Plakate und hängte sie in der Nachbarschaft auf.

Die Leute sahen die Plakate und halfen Lucy bei der Suche. Sie suchten in jeder Straße und fragten jeden, den sie trafen.

Schließlich erkannte jemand den Welpen. Sie kannten den Besitzer und riefen ihn an.

Der Besitzer des Welpen war sehr glücklich, sein Haustier wiederzufinden. Er dankte Lucy für ihre Freundlichkeit und Hilfe.

Lucy umarmte den Welpen zum Abschied. Sie war glücklich, zu sehen, dass der Welpe sicher nach Hause kam.

Vocabulary

Puppy	*Welpe*
Search	*Suchen*
Bark	*Bellen*
Lost	*Verloren*
Poster	*Plakat*
Street	*Straße*
Kind	*Freundlich*
Find	*Finden*
Collar	*Halsband*
Pet	*Haustier*
Happy	*Glücklich*
Home	*Zuhause*
Owner	*Besitzer*
Safe	*Sicher*
Hug	*Umarmung*

Questions About the Story

1. *Why did Lucy decide to search for the puppy's owner?*

    a) She wanted to keep the puppy
    b) The puppy had a collar with a name
    c) She found the puppy lost and kind

2. *What did Lucy do to find the puppy's owner?*

    a) She took the puppy to a vet
    b) She made and put up posters around the neighborhood
    c) She called the police

3. *How did the community respond to Lucy's effort?*

    a) They ignored her
    b) They helped her search for the owner
    c) They advised her to keep the puppy

4. *How was the puppy's owner finally found?*

    a) Through a social media post
    b) Someone recognized the puppy from the posters
    c) The puppy ran back home on its own

5. *What was the puppy's owner's reaction to getting their pet back?*

    a) They were indifferent
    b) They offered a reward to Lucy
    c) They were very happy and thankful

Correct Answers:

1. c) She found the puppy lost and kind
2. b) She made and put up posters around the neighborhood
3. b) They helped her search for the owner
4. b) Someone recognized the puppy from the posters
5. c) They were very happy and thankful

- Chapter Seventeen -
THE ART COMPETITION

Der Kunstwettbewerb

Emma liebte es zu malen. Sie beschloss, an einem Kunstwettbewerb teilzunehmen. Sie nahm ihren Pinsel, Farben und eine große Leinwand, um ihr Bild zu beginnen. Emma wollte etwas voller Farbe und Kreativität schaffen.

Das Thema des Wettbewerbs war "Die Schönheit der Natur." Emma malte eine schöne Landschaft mit Bäumen, einem Fluss und fliegenden Vögeln am Himmel. Sie verwendete leuchtende Farben, um ihr Bild hervorzuheben.

Am Tag der Ausstellung wurde Emmas Gemälde in der Galerie neben vielen anderen ausgestellt. Die Leute kamen, um die Kunst zu sehen und für ihren Favoriten zu stimmen.

Die Richter bewunderten Emmas Design und Kreativität. Als der Gewinner bekannt gegeben wurde, wurde Emmas Name aufgerufen! Sie gewann den Preis für das beste Gemälde.

Emma fühlte sich stolz und glücklich. Ihre Kunst wurde geschätzt, und sie fühlte sich motiviert, noch mehr zu malen.

Vocabulary

Paint	*Malen*
Brush	*Pinsel*
Picture	*Bild*
Color	*Farbe*
Prize	*Preis*
Judge	*Richter*
Exhibit	*Ausstellung*
Creativity	*Kreativität*
Design	*Design*
Art	*Kunst*
Winner	*Gewinner*
Gallery	*Galerie*
Canvas	*Leinwand*
Display	*Ausstellen*
Vote	*Abstimmen*

Questions About the Story

1. *What did Emma decide to do?*

    a) Join a cooking class
    b) Enter an art competition
    c) Write a book

2. *What was the theme of the art competition?*

    a) Modern life
    b) Abstract thoughts
    c) Nature's Beauty

3. *What did Emma paint?*

    a) A cityscape
    b) A portrait
    c) A landscape with trees and a river

4. *What did Emma use to stand out her painting?*

    a) Dark colors
    b) Bright colors
    c) Only black and white

5. *What did the judges admire about Emma's painting?*

    a) The size
    b) The design and creativity
    c) The frame

Correct Answers:

1. b) Enter an art competition
2. c) Nature's Beauty
3. c) A landscape with trees and a river
4. b) Bright colors
5. b) The design and creativity

- Chapter Eighteen -
A DAY AT THE FARM

Ein Tag auf dem Bauernhof

Tom besuchte für einen Tag einen Bauernhof. Er freute sich darauf, alle Tiere zu sehen und mehr über das Landleben zu erfahren. Der Bauer, Herr Brown, hieß Tom willkommen und zeigte ihm alles.

Zuerst gingen sie zur Scheune, um die Kühe und Pferde zu füttern. Tom lernte, wie man eine Kuh melkt, und war von dem Prozess fasziniert. Sie sammelten auch Eier von den Hühnern.

Tom fuhr mit Herrn Brown auf einem Traktor, um die Felder zu sehen. Sie sprachen über die Ernte und wie Heu für die Tiere gemacht wird.

Tom sah Schweine, fütterte sie und half sogar dabei, Heu zu sammeln. Er lernte so viel über die harte Arbeit eines Bauern.

Am Ende des Tages fühlte sich Tom glücklich und dankbar. Er dankte Herrn Brown für die wunderbare Erfahrung auf dem Bauernhof.

Vocabulary

Farm	Bauernhof
Animal	Tier
Cow	Kuh
Horse	Pferd
Feed	Füttern
Barn	Scheune
Tractor	Traktor
Hay	Heu
Milk	Milch
Egg	Ei
Farmer	Bauer
Field	Feld
Harvest	Ernte
Chicken	Huhn
Pig	Schwein

Questions About the Story

1. *Who welcomed Tom to the farm?*

    a) The farm animals
    b) A neighbor
    c) Mr. Brown

2. *What did Tom learn to do for the first time on the farm?*

    a) Drive a tractor
    b) Milk a cow
    c) Ride a horse

3. *What did Tom and Mr. Brown talk about during the tractor ride?*

    a) The weather
    b) The animals' names
    c) The harvest and how hay is made

4. *Besides cows, which other animals did Tom feed?*

    a) Chickens
    b) Pigs
    c) Both chickens and pigs

5. *What was Tom's feeling at the end of his day at the farm?*

    a) Tired
    b) Happy and grateful
    c) Bored

Correct Answers:

1. c) Mr. Brown
2. b) Milk a cow
3. c) The harvest and how hay is made
4. c) Both chickens and pigs
5. b) Happy and grateful

- Chapter Nineteen -
THE SCIENCE FAIR

Der Wissenschaftswettbewerb

Lucy bereitete sich auf den Wissenschaftswettbewerb in ihrer Schule vor. Sie hatte eine großartige Idee für ein Experiment. Ihr Projekt handelte von der chemischen Reaktion zwischen Backpulver und Essig.

Lucy richtete ihre Präsentation im Schul-Labor ein. Sie hatte alle ihre Daten und Beobachtungen bereit, um sie zu präsentieren. Sie war ein wenig nervös, aber auch aufgeregt.

Während des Wettbewerbs kamen viele Schüler und Lehrer, um Lucys Experiment zu sehen. Sie erklärte ihre Hypothese und zeigte ihnen die Reaktion. Alle waren von ihrer Arbeit beeindruckt.

Nachdem alle Projekte getestet und bewertet wurden, verkündeten die Richter die Ergebnisse. Lucys Projekt gewann einen Preis für das beste Experiment!

Lucy war stolz auf ihre harte Arbeit. Der Wissenschaftswettbewerb war ein großer Erfolg, und sie liebte es, ihr Interesse an der Wissenschaft mit anderen zu teilen.

Vocabulary

Experiment	*Experiment*
Science	*Wissenschaft*
Project	*Projekt*
Hypothesis	*Hypothese*
Result	*Ergebnis*
Research	*Forschung*
Display	*Präsentation*
Test	*Testen*
Observation	*Beobachtung*
Conclusion	*Schlussfolgerung*
Data	*Daten*
Measure	*Messen*
Laboratory	*Labor*
Chemical	*Chemisch*
Reaction	*Reaktion*

Questions About the Story

1. *What was Lucy's science fair project about?*

   a) The growth of plants
   b) The solar system
   c) The chemical reaction between baking soda and vinegar

2. *Where did Lucy set up her display for the science fair?*

   a) In the school library
   b) In the school laboratory
   c) In the school gymnasium

3. *How did Lucy feel about presenting her project?*

   a) Confident and bored
   b) Nervous but excited
   c) Indifferent

4. *Who was Lucy's audience during her experiment demonstration?*

   a) Only the judges
   b) Only her classmates
   c) Students and teachers

5. *What did Lucy do during the fair?*

   a) She only observed other projects
   b) She explained her hypothesis and showed the reaction
   c) She helped organize the event

Correct Answers:

1. c) The chemical reaction between baking soda and vinegar
2. b) In the school laboratory
3. b) Nervous but excited
4. c) Students and teachers
5. b) She explained her hypothesis and showed the reaction

- Chapter Twenty -
A SUMMER VACATION

Ein Sommerurlaub

Anna und ihre Familie beschlossen, einen Sommerurlaub zu machen. Sie packten ihre Koffer, trugen Sonnencreme auf und fuhren zum Strand. Es war ein sonniger Tag, perfekt zum Schwimmen und Entspannen.

Sie wohnten in einem kleinen Hotel in der Nähe des Strandes. Jeden Tag erkundeten sie die Insel und entdeckten neue Orte. Anna liebte es, mit ihrer Kamera Fotos zu machen, um sich an das Abenteuer zu erinnern.

Eines Tages beschlossen sie, Souvenirs für ihre Freunde zu kaufen. Sie fanden schöne Muscheln und Postkarten. Anna wählte ein kleines, handgemachtes Boot als Erinnerung an ihre Reise.

Abends saßen sie am Strand und beobachteten die Sterne. Anna fühlte sich glücklich und entspannt. Dieser Urlaub war ein Abenteuer, das sie nie vergessen würde.

Vocabulary

Vacation	*Urlaub*
Beach	*Strand*
Travel	*Reisen*
Suitcase	*Koffer*
Hotel	*Hotel*
Sunscreen	*Sonnencreme*
Swim	*Schwimmen*
Map	*Karte*
Tourist	*Tourist*
Relax	*Entspannen*
Explore	*Erkunden*
Adventure	*Abenteuer*
Souvenir	*Souvenir*
Island	*Insel*
Camera	*Kamera*

Questions About the Story

1. *What did Anna and her family do during their summer vacation?*

    a) Went skiing
    b) Went to the beach
    c) Visited a museum

2. *What did Anna use to capture memories of their vacation?*

    a) Her memory
    b) A diary
    c) A camera

3. *What type of souvenirs did Anna and her family buy?*

    a) Magnets and keychains
    b) Shells and postcards
    c) T-shirts and hats

4. *What was Anna's special souvenir from the trip?*

    a) A seashell necklace
    b) A beach towel
    c) A small, handmade boat

5. *Where did Anna and her family stay during their vacation?*

    a) In a tent
    b) In a large resort
    c) In a small hotel near the beach

Correct Answers:

1. b) Went to the beach
2. c) A camera
3. b) Shells and postcards
4. c) A small, handmade boat
5. c) In a small hotel near the beach

- Chapter Twenty-One -
THE BICYCLE RACE

Das Fahrradrennen

Mike trat in seiner Stadt in ein Fahrradrennen ein. Er setzte seinen Helm auf, überprüfte die Reifen seines Fahrrads und stellte sicher, dass er die richtige Ausrüstung für die Geschwindigkeit hatte. Die Rennstrecke war lang und herausfordernd, aber Mike war bereit zu konkurrieren.

Als das Rennen begann, trat Mike so schnell er konnte in die Pedale. Er spürte den Wind in seinem Gesicht und die Aufregung des Wettbewerbs. Er konzentrierte sich auf die Ziellinie und versuchte, seine Energie hoch zu halten.

Um ihn herum gaben auch die anderen Radfahrer ihr Bestes. Mike wusste, dass er seine Geschwindigkeit halten musste, um zu gewinnen. Als sie sich der Ziellinie näherten, gab Mike alles und überquerte die Linie als Erster.

Er hatte das Rennen gewonnen! Mike fühlte sich stolz und glücklich. Er war nun der Champion des Fahrradrennens.

Vocabulary

Bicycle	*Fahrrad*
Race	*Rennen*
Helmet	*Helm*
Pedal	*Pedal*
Speed	*Geschwindigkeit*
Track	*Strecke*
Compete	*Konkurrieren*
Finish line	*Ziellinie*
Tire	*Reifen*
Champion	*Champion*
Route	*Route*
Energy	*Energie*
Cyclist	*Radfahrer*
Gear	*Ausrüstung*
Victory	*Sieg*

Questions About the Story

1. *What did Mike do to prepare for the bicycle race?*

    a) Checked his bicycle's tires
    b) Put on his running shoes
    c) Packed a lunch

2. *What was Mike's feeling during the race?*

    a) Scared
    b) Excited
    c) Tired

3. *How did Mike feel about the race track?*

    a) Easy
    b) Boring
    c) Long and challenging

4. *What was essential for Mike to win the race?*

    a) Speed
    b) A new bike
    c) A cheering crowd

5. *What did Mike focus on to keep his energy high?*

    a) The start line
    b) The other cyclists
    c) The finish line

Correct Answers:

1. a) Checked his bicycle's tires
2. b) Excited
3. c) Long and challenging
4. a) Speed
5. c) The finish line

- Chapter Twenty-Two -
A NIGHT AT THE CAMPING

Eine Nacht beim Camping

Sarah und ihre Freunde gingen im Wald zelten. Sie stellten ihr Zelt neben einem wunderschönen See auf. Als die Nacht hereinbrach, entzündeten sie ein Lagerfeuer und rösteten Marshmallows.

Der Wald war still, und der Himmel war voller Sterne. Sie erzählten sich Geschichten und genossen die Ruhe der Natur. Sarah war glücklich, fernab der geschäftigen Stadt zu sein.

Bevor sie schlafen gingen, schalteten sie ihre Taschenlampen ein, um den Weg zurück zum Zelt zu finden. Die Nacht war dunkel, aber das Feuer hielt sie warm.

Im Zelt liegend, lauschten sie den Geräuschen des Waldes. Es war eine perfekte Nacht zum Zelten. Sarah dachte darüber nach, wie sehr sie die Ruhe und die Sterne liebte.

Vocabulary

Camping	Camping
Tent	Zelt
Fire	Feuer
Marshmallow	Marshmallow
Forest	Wald
Star	Stern
Sleep	Schlafen
Dark	Dunkel
Flashlight	Taschenlampe
Backpack	Rucksack
Nature	Natur
Quiet	Still
Campfire	Lagerfeuer
Night	Nacht
Lake	See

Questions About the Story

1. *What did Sarah and her friends do as night fell during their camping trip?*

   a) They went to sleep immediately
   b) They lit a campfire and roasted marshmallows
   c) They packed up and went home

2. *What made Sarah feel happy while camping?*

   a) The busy city life
   b) The sound of cars passing by
   c) The peacefulness of nature

3. *What did Sarah and her friends use to find their way back to the tent?*

   a) A map
   b) Flashlights
   c) A compass

4. *How did Sarah and her friends feel about the forest at night?*

   a) Scared and uneasy
   b) Curious and adventurous
   c) Peaceful and content

5. *What kept Sarah and her friends warm at night?*

   a) Their sleeping bags
   b) The campfire
   c) Hot drinks

Correct Answers:

1. b) They lit a campfire and roasted marshmallows
2. c) The peacefulness of nature
3. b) Flashlights
4. c) Peaceful and content
5. b) The campfire

- Chapter Twenty-Three -
THE FAMILY REUNION

Das Familientreffen

Letzten Sommer besuchte Emma ein Familientreffen. Es wurde im Haus ihrer Großeltern abgehalten, wo sich alle Verwandten, einschließlich Cousins, Tanten und Onkel, versammelten. Sie organisierten ein großes Grillfest im Garten.

Alle lachten und teilten Geschichten aus der Vergangenheit. Emmas Großeltern erzählten Anekdoten aus ihrer Jugend, die alle amüsant und herzerwärmend fanden. Es gab Umarmungen und Lächeln überall, als die Familienmitglieder wieder zusammenkamen.

Sie machten viele Fotos, um die Erinnerungen an den Tag festzuhalten. Das Treffen war eine Feier der familiären Bande und Liebe. Sie genossen ein Festmahl zusammen und spürten die Freude, nach langer Zeit wieder vereint zu sein.

Emma war dankbar für ihre Familie. Das Treffen erinnerte sie an die starke Bindung, die sie teilten. Sie freute sich auf weitere Zusammenkünfte in der Zukunft.

Vocabulary

Family	Familie
Reunion	Treffen
Cousin	Cousin
Barbecue	Grillen
Laugh	Lachen
Story	Geschichte
Grandparent	Großelternteil
Hug	Umarmung
Together	Zusammen
Memory	Erinnerung
Photo	Foto
Celebration	Feier
Feast	Festmahl
Joy	Freude
Relative	Verwandter

Questions About the Story

1. *Where was the family reunion held?*

   a) At a park
   b) At Emma's house
   c) At her grandparents' house

2. *What did the family organize in the garden?*

   a) A dance party
   b) A big barbecue
   c) A swimming competition

3. *What were Emma's grandparents doing that everyone found amusing?*

   a) Performing magic tricks
   b) Singing
   c) Telling tales about their youth

4. *How did the family members feel during the reunion?*

   a) Indifferent
   b) Anxious
   c) Joyful and grateful

5. *What did Emma and her family do to capture memories of the day?*

   a) Painted a mural
   b) Wrote in a journal
   c) Took a lot of photos

Correct Answers:

1. c) At her grandparents' house
2. b) A big barbecue
3. c) Telling tales about their youth
4. c) Joyful and grateful
5. c) Took a lot of photos

- Chapter Twenty-Four -
A VISIT TO THE MUSEUM

Ein Besuch im Museum

Liam und seine Klasse machten einen Ausflug ins Museum. Sie waren gespannt darauf, die Ausstellungen über Geschichte und Kunst zu sehen. Der Museumsführer führte sie durch die Galerien und erklärte jede Ausstellung.

Sie sahen antike Skulpturen und schöne Gemälde. Liam war fasziniert von den Geschichten hinter jedem Kunstwerk. Sie lernten über verschiedene Kulturen und entdeckten Informationen, die ihnen neu waren.

Eines der Highlights war das Sehen einer Statue aus einer antiken Zivilisation. Liam machte Notizen und stellte dem Führer viele Fragen. Er wollte so viel wie möglich lernen.

Der Museumsbesuch war ein bildungsreiches Abenteuer. Liam und seine Klassenkameraden verließen das Museum inspiriert und waren begierig darauf, mehr über Geschichte und Kunst zu erfahren.

Vocabulary

Museum	*Museum*
Exhibit	*Ausstellung*
History	*Geschichte*
Art	*Kunst*
Guide	*Führer*
Sculpture	*Skulptur*
Painting	*Gemälde*
Ticket	*Ticket*
Tour	*Tour*
Ancient	*Antik*
Culture	*Kultur*
Discover	*Entdecken*
Information	*Information*
Statue	*Statue*
Gallery	*Galerie*

Questions About the Story

1. *What was the purpose of Liam and his class's visit to the museum?*

    a) To see exhibits about history and art
    b) To participate in an art competition
    c) To attend a music concert

2. *Who led Liam and his class through the museum?*

    a) Their teacher
    b) A museum guide
    c) A famous artist

3. *What did Liam find fascinating at the museum?*

    a) Modern art installations
    b) Ancient sculptures and beautiful paintings
    c) Interactive science exhibits

4. *What did Liam do when he saw the statue from an ancient civilization?*

    a) He ignored it
    b) He took notes and asked many questions
    c) He drew a sketch of it

5. *What did Liam and his classmates learn about at the museum?*

    a) Different cultures
    b) Cooking recipes
    c) Sports history

Correct Answers:

1. a) To see exhibits about history and art
2. b) A museum guide
3. b) Ancient sculptures and beautiful paintings
4. b) He took notes and asked many questions
5. a) Different cultures

- Chapter Twenty-Five -
THE BOOK CLUB

Der Buchclub

Anna trat einem Buchclub in ihrer Nachbarschaft bei. Jeden Monat wählen sie einen Roman, den sie lesen und diskutieren. Diesen Monat lasen sie eine faszinierende Geschichte mit interessanten Charakteren und einer komplexen Handlung.

Beim Treffen teilten die Mitglieder ihre Meinungen und Interpretationen des Buches. Sie sprachen über den Stil des Autors und die Themen, die in der Geschichte erkundet wurden. Jeder hatte unterschiedliche Ansichten, was die Diskussion lebendig und interessant machte.

Anna genoss es, die Gedanken der anderen über das Buch zu hören. Es war für sie aufschlussreich zu sehen, wie eine Geschichte auf so viele Arten wahrgenommen werden konnte. Der Club empfahl auch andere Bücher desselben Autors und ähnlicher Genres.

Die Teilnahme am Buchclub ermöglichte es Anna, neue Literatur zu entdecken und Freunde zu finden, die ihre Leidenschaft für das Lesen teilten. Sie freute sich auf jedes Treffen und die neuen Bücher, die sie gemeinsam erkunden würden.

Vocabulary

Book	*Buch*
Club	*Club*
Read	*Lesen*
Discuss	*Diskutieren*
Author	*Autor*
Novel	*Roman*
Character	*Charakter*
Plot	*Handlung*
Meeting	*Treffen*
Opinion	*Meinung*
Chapter	*Kapitel*
Recommend	*Empfehlen*
Genre	*Genre*
Theme	*Thema*
Literature	*Literatur*

Questions About the Story

1. What activity does Anna participate in with her neighborhood?

   a) Gardening
   b) Painting
   c) Reading books

2. How often does the book club choose a new novel to read?

   a) Every month
   b) Every week
   c) Every two months

3. What did the book club members do at the meeting?

   a) Practiced cooking
   b) Shared their opinions about the book
   c) Painted pictures

4. How did Anna feel about the book club discussions?

   a) Enlightened and interested
   b) Bored and uninterested
   c) Confused and overwhelmed

5. What did the book club do besides discussing the current book?

   a) Organized a picnic
   b) Took a group photo
   c) Recommended other books

Correct Answers:

1. c) Reading books
2. a) Every month
3. b) Shared their opinions about the book
4. a) Enlightened and interested
5. c) Recommended other books

- Chapter Twenty-Six -
SPORTS DAY

Sporttag

Heute ist Sporttag in der Schule. Alle sind aufgeregt wegen des Wettbewerbs. Die Teams sind bereit, und die Athleten wärmen sich auf der Bahn auf. Die Luft ist erfüllt vom Klang der anfeuernden Menschen.

Das erste Ereignis ist das Rennen. Mark läuft so schnell er kann, seine Augen auf die Ziellinie gerichtet. Er gewinnt das Rennen und ist stolz, als er eine Medaille erhält. Sein Trainer gibt ihm ein Daumen hoch, und sein Team jubelt laut.

Als nächstes ist der Weitsprung dran. Sarah atmet tief ein und läuft. Sie springt mit all ihrer Kraft und gewinnt eine weitere Medaille für ihr Team. Jeder applaudiert ihrer Leistung.

Am Ende des Tages gewinnt das Team mit den meisten Medaillen die Trophäe. Sie haben hart für diesen Tag trainiert, und ihre Anstrengung hat sich ausgezahlt. Der Sporttag war ein Erfolg, voller Spaß, Wettbewerb und Teamgeist.

Vocabulary

Competition	*Wettbewerb*
Team	*Team*
Medal	*Medaille*
Race	*Rennen*
Jump	*Springen*
Run	*Laufen*
Winner	*Gewinner*
Coach	*Trainer*
Sport	*Sport*
Cheer	*Anfeuern*
Athlete	*Athlet*
Track	*Bahn*
Strength	*Kraft*
Practice	*Üben*
Trophy	*Trophäe*

Questions About the Story

1. *What event did Mark participate in during Sports Day?*

    a) Race
    b) Long jump
    c) Soccer

2. *Who won the race?*

    a) Sarah
    b) The coach
    c) Mark

3. *What did Mark feel after winning the race?*

    a) Sad
    b) Proud and happy
    c) Indifferent

4. *What event did Sarah win?*

    a) Race
    b) Long jump
    c) Chess

5. *What did the team win at the end of the day?*

    a) A medal
    b) A trophy
    c) A certificate

Correct Answers:

1. a) Race
2. c) Mark
3. b) Proud and happy
4. b) Long jump
5. b) A trophy

- Chapter Twenty-Seven -
THE MAGIC SHOW

Die Zaubershow

Heute Abend findet im Rathaus eine Zaubershow statt. Der Zauberer Leo ist bereit, sein Publikum mit Tricks und Illusionen zu verblüffen. Der Raum ist dunkel, abgesehen vom Scheinwerferlicht auf der Bühne.

Leo beginnt damit, einen Hasen aus seinem Hut verschwinden zu lassen. Das Publikum keucht überrascht und applaudiert dann. Für seinen nächsten Trick bittet er einen Freiwilligen, eine Karte zu ziehen. Die gewählte Karte erscheint magisch in Leos Tasche!

Der letzte Akt ist der spektakulärste. Leo schwingt seinen Zauberstab und mit einem "Puff" verschwindet er, um hinter dem Publikum wieder aufzutauchen! Alle sind verblüfft und jubeln laut.

Als der Vorhang fällt, applaudiert das Publikum weiterhin, erstaunt über die Magie, die sie erlebt haben. Es war ein Abend voller Überraschungen und bezaubernder Illusionen.

Vocabulary

Magic	*Magie*
Trick	*Trick*
Magician	*Zauberer*
Disappear	*Verschwinden*
Rabbit	*Hase*
Hat	*Hut*
Applaud	*Applaudieren*
Card	*Karte*
Illusion	*Illusion*
Show	*Show*
Wand	*Zauberstab*
Audience	*Publikum*
Perform	*Aufführen*
Curtain	*Vorhang*
Surprise	*Überraschung*

Questions About the Story

1. *Where was the magic show hosted?*

    a) School auditorium
    b) Town hall
    c) Local park

2. *What was the first trick Leo performed?*

    a) Pulled a rabbit from his hat
    b) Made himself disappear
    c) Picked a card from a volunteer

3. *How did Leo surprise the audience with the card trick?*

    a) The card floated in mid-air
    b) The card changed colors
    c) The chosen card appeared in his pocket

4. *What was Leo's final act?*

    a) Turning day into night
    b) Making a volunteer vanish
    c) Disappearing and reappearing behind the audience

5. *How did the audience react to Leo's final act?*

    a) With silence
    b) With boos
    c) With loud cheers

Correct Answers:

1. b) Town hall
2. a) Pulled a rabbit from his hat
3. c) The chosen card appeared in his pocket
4. c) Disappearing and reappearing behind the audience
5. c) With loud cheers

- Chapter Twenty-Eight -
AT THE BEACH

Am Strand

Emma und ihre Freunde beschließen, den Tag am Strand zu verbringen. Die Sonne scheint und eine sanfte Brise kühlt die Luft. Sie breiten ihre Handtücher auf dem weichen Sand aus und richten einen Sonnenschirm auf.

Die Kinder bauen nahe am Ufer eine Sandburg, während Emma und ihre Freunde sich sonnen und plaudern. Sie beobachten die fliegenden Möwen und lauschen dem Rauschen der Wellen.

Nach einer Weile gehen alle schwimmen. Das Wasser ist erfrischend. Sie planschen und spielen in den Wellen, lachen und haben eine großartige Zeit.

Als der Tag endet, packen sie ihre Sachen zusammen und hinterlassen Fußspuren im Sand. Der Tag am Strand war perfekt, voller Spaß, Entspannung und der Schönheit der Natur.

Vocabulary

Sand	*Sand*
Wave	*Welle*
Shell	*Muschel*
Towel	*Handtuch*
Sunbathe	*Sonnenbaden*
Castle	*Burg*
Ocean	*Ozean*
Seagull	*Möwe*
Shore	*Ufer*
Swim	*Schwimmen*
Bucket	*Eimer*
Sunburn	*Sonnenbrand*
Surf	*Surfen*
Cool	*Kühl*
Breeze	*Brise*

Questions About the Story

1. **What did Emma and her friends decide to do for the day?**

    a) Go hiking
    b) Visit the museum
    c) Spend the day at the beach

2. **What activity did the children engage in near the shore?**

    a) Playing volleyball
    b) Building a sandcastle
    c) Swimming

3. **What did Emma and her friends do while the children played?**

    a) They went for a swim
    b) They built a sandcastle
    c) They sunbathed and chatted

4. **How did Emma and her friends feel when they went for a swim?**

    a) Tired
    b) Cold
    c) Refreshed

5. **What did they do as the day ended?**

    a) Started a campfire
    b) Left footprints in the sand as they packed up
    c) Stayed for the night

Correct Answers:

1. c) Spend the day at the beach
2. b) Building a sandcastle
3. c) They sunbathed and chatted
4. c) Refreshed
5. b) Left footprints in the sand as they packed up

- Chapter Twenty-Nine -
THE PHOTOGRAPHY CONTEST

Der Fotowettbewerb

Anna liebt es, Fotos zu machen. Sie erfährt von einem Fotowettbewerb in ihrer Stadt. Das Thema ist „Natur in der Stadt". Anna ist aufgeregt und möchte das perfekte Bild einfangen.

Sie nimmt ihre Kamera und läuft durch die Stadt. Anna sucht nach dem besten Winkel, um die Natur in der belebten Stadt zu zeigen. Sie fotografiert Bäume im Park, Vögel auf der Straße und Blumen, die durch Risse im Gehweg wachsen.

Nach vielen Aufnahmen wählt Anna ihr bestes Bild aus. Es ist ein Foto eines Schmetterlings auf einer Blume mit Wolkenkratzern im Hintergrund. Sie bearbeitet das Foto, um den Schmetterling stärker hervorzuheben, und reicht es beim Wettbewerb ein.

Wochen später erhält Anna großartige Neuigkeiten. Sie ist die Gewinnerin! Ihr Bild wird im Rathaus ausgestellt. Sie gewinnt einen Preis und ist stolz auf ihre Arbeit. Anna ist glücklich, dass sie die Schönheit der Natur in der Stadt durch ihre Linse zeigen konnte.

Vocabulary

Camera	*Kamera*
Photograph	*Fotografieren*
Picture	*Bild*
Contest	*Wettbewerb*
Image	*Bild*
Focus	*Fokus*
Prize	*Preis*
Capture	*Einfangen*
Lens	*Linse*
Angle	*Winkel*
Shot	*Aufnahme*
Edit	*Bearbeiten*
Theme	*Thema*
Winner	*Gewinner*
Exhibit	*Ausstellen*

Questions About the Story

1. *What is the theme of the photography contest Anna participates in?*

   a) Urban Landscapes
   b) Nature in the City
   c) City Nightlife

2. *What subjects does Anna photograph for the contest?*

   a) Skyscrapers and streets
   b) People in the city
   c) Trees, birds, and flowers

3. *What makes Anna's winning photograph special?*

   a) It shows a crowded city scene
   b) It captures a butterfly on a flower with skyscrapers in the background
   c) It is a picture of a sunset over the city

4. *How does Anna feel after winning the photography contest?*

   a) Disappointed
   b) Confused
   c) Proud

5. *What does Anna do with her camera in the city?*

   a) Sells it
   b) Takes photographs
   c) Loses it

Correct Answers:

1. b) Nature in the City
2. c) Trees, birds, and flowers
3. b) It captures a butterfly on a flower with skyscrapers in the background
4. c) Proud
5. b) Takes photographs

- Chapter Thirty -
A PLAY IN THE PARK

Ein Theaterstück im Park

Die lokale Theatergruppe beschließt, ein Theaterstück im Park aufzuführen. Das Stück ist eine Komödie über Freundschaft und Abenteuer. Alle freuen sich auf die Aufführung im Freien.

Lucas ist der Regisseur. Er arbeitet mit den Schauspielern daran, ihre Texte und Aktionen zu proben. Die Schauspieler tragen farbenfrohe Kostüme und verwenden Requisiten, um die Szenen interessanter zu gestalten.

Am Tag der Aufführung kommen viele Menschen in den Park. Sie sitzen auf Decken und Stühlen und warten darauf, dass das Stück beginnt. Wenn sich der Vorhang öffnet, erscheinen die Schauspieler auf der Bühne und das Stück beginnt.

Das Publikum genießt das Stück. Sie lachen und applaudieren nach jeder Szene. Die Schauspieler freuen sich, so vielen Menschen Freude zu bereiten.

Nach der letzten Szene spendet das Publikum großen Applaus. Die Schauspieler verbeugen sich, und Lucas bedankt sich bei allen für ihr Kommen. Es war ein erfolgreiches Theaterstück im Park, und alle hoffen, in Zukunft mehr zu sehen.

Vocabulary

Play	*Theaterstück*
Actor	*Schauspieler*
Stage	*Bühne*
Performance	*Aufführung*
Audience	*Publikum*
Script	*Skript*
Character	*Charakter*
Applause	*Applaus*
Costume	*Kostüm*
Rehearse	*Proben*
Director	*Regisseur*
Curtain	*Vorhang*
Drama	*Drama*
Props	*Requisiten*
Scene	*Szene*

Questions About the Story

1. *What type of play does the local theater group decide to perform in the park?*

    a) A drama about history
    b) A comedy about friendship and adventure
    c) A musical about love

2. *Who is the director of the play?*

    a) Lucas
    b) Emma
    c) Sarah

3. *What do the actors use to make the scenes more interesting?*

    a) Special lighting effects
    b) Colorful costumes and props
    c) Pre-recorded music

4. *How does the audience watch the play?*

    a) Standing up
    b) Sitting on blankets and chairs
    c) Via a live stream

5. *What is the audience's reaction to the play?*

    a) They are bored
    b) They are confused
    c) They laugh and applaud

Correct Answers:

1. b) A comedy about friendship and adventure
2. a) Lucas
3. b) Colorful costumes and props
4. b) Sitting on blankets and chairs
5. c) They laugh and applaud

- Chapter Thirty-One -
THE HEALTH FAIR

Der Gesundheitstag

Das Gemeindezentrum organisiert einen Gesundheitstag. Ziel ist es, die Menschen über Ernährung, Bewegung und allgemeines Wohlbefinden zu informieren. Viele Ärzte und Experten kommen, um Ratschläge zu geben und kostenlose Untersuchungen durchzuführen.

Emily möchte mehr über gesundes Leben erfahren. Sie besucht verschiedene Stände auf der Messe. An einem Stand lernt sie die Bedeutung von Bewegung kennen. Ein anderer Stand bietet Ernährungsberatung für eine ausgewogene Ernährung an.

Es gibt auch Screenings für verschiedene Gesundheitschecks. Emily entscheidet sich für eine Untersuchung, und der Arzt sagt ihr, dass sie gesund ist, aber regelmäßiger Sport treiben sollte.

Emily verlässt den Gesundheitstag motiviert. Sie hat viel darüber gelernt, wie sie ihren Körper gesund halten kann. Sie plant, mehr Sport zu treiben und sich besser zu ernähren. Der Gesundheitstag war ein großartiger Weg für sie, ihre Reise zur Wellness zu beginnen.

Vocabulary

Health	Gesundheit
Fair	Messe
Nutrition	Ernährung
Exercise	Bewegung
Doctor	Arzt
Check-up	Untersuchung
Wellness	Wohlbefinden
Booth	Stand
Advice	Rat
Fitness	Fitness
Screen	Screening
Healthy	Gesund
Diet	Diät
Prevention	Prävention
Hygiene	Hygiene

Questions About the Story

1. *Where did the health fair take place?*

    a) At a school
    b) In a park
    c) At the community center

2. *What was the main goal of the health fair?*

    a) To promote local businesses
    b) To teach people about nutrition, exercise, and wellness
    c) To fundraise for the community center

3. *Which booth did Emily learn about the importance of exercise?*

    a) Nutrition booth
    b) Exercise booth
    c) Wellness booth

4. *What advice did another booth offer Emily?*

    a) To exercise more regularly
    b) To drink more water
    c) Nutritional advice for a balanced diet

5. *What did the doctor advise Emily after her health check-up?*

    a) She's healthy but should exercise more regularly
    b) She needs to eat more vegetables
    c) She should drink more water

Correct Answers:

1. c) At the community center
2. b) To teach people about nutrition, exercise, and wellness
3. b) Exercise booth
4. c) Nutritional advice for a balanced diet
5. a) She's healthy but should exercise more regularly

- Chapter Thirty-Two -
A BOAT TRIP

Eine Bootsfahrt

Tom und seine Freunde beschließen, eine Bootsfahrt auf dem Fluss zu machen. Tom ist der Kapitän des kleinen Bootes. Sie tragen Schwimmwesten zur Sicherheit und starten ihre Reise früh am Morgen.

Das Wasser ist ruhig, und sie sehen Fische unter dem Boot schwimmen. Die Sonne scheint hell und lässt das Wasser funkeln. Sie segeln an grünen Ufern vorbei und winken anderen Booten zu.

Mittags ankern sie an einem schönen Ort und machen ein Picknick auf dem Deck. Sie teilen Sandwiches und Getränke, genießen die Aussicht und die sanften Wellen.

Nach der Pause setzen sie ihre Fahrt fort. Sie sehen Vögel über den Fluss fliegen und genießen die frische Luft. Die Reise fühlt sich wie ein Abenteuer an.

Als die Sonne untergeht, kehren sie zum Hafen zurück und legen das Boot an. Sie danken Tom dafür, dass er ein großartiger Kapitän war. Es war ein perfekter Tag auf dem Wasser, voller Spaß und Entspannung.

Vocabulary

Boat	*Boot*
River	*Fluss*
Sail	*Segeln*
Captain	*Kapitän*
Fish	*Fisch*
Water	*Wasser*
Trip	*Reise*
Anchor	*Anker*
Deck	*Deck*
Wave	*Welle*
Life jacket	*Schwimmweste*
Port	*Hafen*
Voyage	*Fahrt*
Crew	*Mannschaft*
Dock	*Anlegen*

Questions About the Story

1. *Who is the captain of the boat during the trip?*

   a) Tom
   b) One of Tom's friends
   c) A hired captain

2. *What safety gear did Tom and his friends wear on the boat?*

   a) Life jackets
   b) Helmets
   c) Elbow pads

3. *What time of day did they start their boat trip?*

   a) Early in the morning
   b) At noon
   c) In the evening

4. *What natural feature did they enjoy during their picnic on the deck?*

   a) Mountains
   b) Fish swimming under the boat
   c) Desert

5. *What did Tom and his friends do at noon during their boat trip?*

   a) Continued sailing
   b) Went swimming
   c) Had a picnic on the deck

Correct Answers:

1. a) Tom
2. a) Life jackets
3. a) Early in the morning
4. b) Fish swimming under the boat
5. c) Had a picnic on the deck

- Chapter Thirty-Three -
THE SCHOOL CONCERT

Das Schulkonzert

Die Schule beschließt, ein Konzert zu veranstalten, um ihre Musikband und den Chor zu präsentieren. Die Schüler haben wochenlang geprobt, und alle freuen sich darauf aufzutreten.

Am Abend des Konzerts füllt sich das Auditorium der Schule. Die Lichter dimmen, und die Bühne erleuchtet. Die Band beginnt zu spielen, und die Sänger beginnen zu singen. Die Musik erfüllt den Raum, und das Publikum ist gefesselt.

Während des Konzerts führen mehrere Schüler Solos auf. Sie spielen Instrumente oder singen und zeigen ihr Talent. Nach jeder Aufführung applaudiert das Publikum laut und zeigt seine Anerkennung.

Das letzte Lied bringt alle auf der Bühne zusammen. Es ist ein schöner Moment, und wenn die Musik endet, ist der Applaus donnernd.

Das Konzert war ein Erfolg. Die Schüler sind stolz auf ihre Leistung, und das Publikum verlässt den Raum summend zum letzten Lied. Es war eine Nacht, die man sich merken wird, voller Musik und Freude.

Vocabulary

Concert	*Konzert*
Music	*Musik*
Band	*Band*
Sing	*Singen*
Audience	*Publikum*
Stage	*Bühne*
Instrument	*Instrument*
Perform	*Auftreten*
Choir	*Chor*
Song	*Lied*
Applause	*Applaus*
Microphone	*Mikrofon*
Rehearsal	*Probe*
Solo	*Solo*
Note	*Note*

Questions About the Story

1. *What event does the story describe?*

   a) A school play
   b) A school concert
   c) A sports day

2. *What did the students do to prepare for the concert?*

   a) Practiced for weeks
   b) Studied science experiments
   c) Rehearsed a play

3. *How did the audience react to the concert?*

   a) They were silent
   b) They left early
   c) They applauded loudly

4. *What was the highlight of the concert?*

   a) The lighting
   b) The solos
   c) The costumes

5. *What brought everyone together on stage?*

   a) The opening song
   b) The final song
   c) An award ceremony

Correct Answers:

1. b) A school concert
2. a) Practiced for weeks
3. c) They applauded loudly
4. b) The solos
5. b) The final song

- Chapter Thirty-Four -
A WINTER FESTIVAL

Das Winterfest

Die Stadt veranstaltet jedes Jahr ein Winterfest. Dieses Jahr beschließen Lucy und ihre Familie, sich dem Spaß anzuschließen. Das Fest bietet viele Aktivitäten wie Eislaufen, Schneeballschlachten und das Trinken von heißem Kakao.

Sie beginnen mit dem Schlittschuhlaufen auf dem zugefrorenen Teich. Lucy ist anfangs etwas ungeschickt, aber bald gleitet sie wie eine Profi. Sie lachen und genießen die frische Winterluft.

Als Nächstes veranstalten sie eine Schneeballschlacht und bauen Forts aus Schnee. Die Schneeflocken fallen sanft und erhöhen den Spaß. Nach der Schlacht wärmen sie sich mit heißem Kakao am Kamin auf und fühlen sich gemütlich.

Der Höhepunkt des Festes ist die Schlittenfahrt. Sie wickeln sich in Schals und Fäustlinge und genießen die Fahrt durch die verschneiten Straßen, spüren die Kälte, aber lieben die Wärme des Zusammenseins.

Das Winterfest bringt Freude und Wärme in die kalte Jahreszeit. Lucy und ihre Familie gehen glücklich und zufrieden nach Hause und freuen sich schon auf das nächste Jahr.

Vocabulary

Festival	*Festival*
Ice skating	*Schlittschuhlaufen*
Snowball	*Schneeball*
Hot cocoa	*Heißer Kakao*
Winter	*Winter*
Snowflake	*Schneeflocke*
Mittens	*Fäustlinge*
Scarf	*Schal*
Fireplace	*Kamin*
Celebration	*Feier*
Chill	*Kälte*
Sleigh	*Schlitten*
Frost	*Frost*
Warmth	*Wärme*
Cozy	*Gemütlich*

Questions About the Story

1. *What is the theme of the winter festival?*

   a) Sports competitions
   b) Food tasting
   c) Ice skating and snow activities

2. *What activity did Lucy find challenging at first?*

   a) Sleigh riding
   b) Snowball fighting
   c) Ice skating

3. *How did Lucy and her family feel during the sleigh ride?*

   a) Scared
   b) Excited but cold
   c) Bored

4. *What did Lucy and her family do to warm up after the snowball fight?*

   a) Went home
   b) Drank hot cocoa by the fireplace
   c) Continued playing in the snow

5. *What makes the winter festival special for Lucy and her family?*

   a) Winning a prize
   b) The cold weather
   c) The joy and warmth of being together

Correct Answers:

1. c) Ice skating and snow activities
2. c) Ice skating
3. b) Excited but cold
4. b) Drank hot cocoa by the fireplace
5. c) The joy and warmth of being together

- Chapter Thirty-Five -
THE HOMEMADE ROBOT

Der selbstgemachte Roboter

Jake liebt es, Dinge zu erfinden. Eines Tages beschließt er, einen Roboter zu bauen. Er sammelt Batterien, Drähte und andere Teile. Er arbeitet in seinem Zimmer, entwirft und programmiert seinen neuen Freund.

Nach vielen Stunden ist Jakes Roboter fertig. Er nennt ihn Robo. Robo kann sich bewegen, sprechen und sogar bei den Hausaufgaben helfen. Jake bedient Robo mit einer Fernsteuerung und zeigt ihm das Haus.

Jakes Familie ist von Robo begeistert. Sie sehen zu, wie Robo Spielzeug aufhebt und das Zimmer reinigt. Jake ist stolz auf seine Erfindung. Er plant weitere Experimente, um Robos Funktionen zu verbessern.

Robo wird ein Teil von Jakes Familie. Jake lernt viel über Technologie und Maschinen durch Robo. Er träumt davon, ein großer Erfinder zu werden und mehr Roboter zu erschaffen, die den Menschen helfen.

Vocabulary

Robot	Roboter
Build	Bauen
Program	Programmieren
Battery	Batterie
Control	Steuern
Invent	Erfinden
Machine	Maschine
Design	Entwerfen
Circuit	Schaltkreis
Technology	Technologie
Sensor	Sensor
Operate	Bedienen
Experiment	Experiment
Function	Funktion
Automatic	Automatisch

Questions About the Story

1. *What does Jake love to do?*

    a) Cook
    b) Invent things
    c) Play sports

2. *What is the name of Jake's robot?*

    a) Robo
    b) Buddy
    c) Sparky

3. *What can Robo do?*

    a) Sing
    b) Dance
    c) Help with homework

4. *How does Jake operate Robo?*

    a) Voice commands
    b) A remote control
    c) An app

5. *What is Jake's family's reaction to Robo?*

    a) Scared
    b) Amazed
    c) Indifferent

Correct Answers:

1. b) Invent things
2. a) Robo
3. c) Help with homework
4. b) A remote control
5. b) Amazed

- Chapter Thirty-Six -
A SCIENCE EXPERIMENT

Ein naturwissenschaftliches Experiment

Sara ist eine neugierige Schülerin, die Wissenschaft liebt. Für ihr Schulprojekt entscheidet sie sich, ein Experiment im Labor durchzuführen. Sie möchte chemische Reaktionen verstehen.

Mit Schutzbrillen ausgestattet misst Sara sorgfältig Chemikalien ab und gießt sie in ein Reagenzglas. Sie beobachtet, wie sich die Lösung verfärbt und Blasen bilden. Sie notiert ihre Beobachtungen und Hypothesen.

Ihr Lehrer sieht zu und nickt zustimmend. Sara erklärt ihr Experiment der Klasse und zeigt ihre Daten und Ergebnisse. Ihre Freunde sind beeindruckt von ihrem Wissen und der spannenden Reaktion.

Saras Experiment gewinnt den Schulwissenschaftswettbewerb. Sie ist stolz und begeistert über ihre Leistung. Sie erkennt, dass Wissenschaft darin besteht, die Wunder der Welt zu erforschen und zu entdecken.

Vocabulary

Experiment	*Experiment*
Science	*Wissenschaft*
Test tube	*Reagenzglas*
Measure	*Messen*
Observation	*Beobachtung*
Laboratory	*Labor*
Chemical	*Chemikalie*
Reaction	*Reaktion*
Hypothesis	*Hypothese*
Data	*Daten*
Result	*Ergebnis*
Research	*Forschung*
Safety goggles	*Schutzbrillen*
Solution	*Lösung*
Analyze	*Analysieren*

Questions About the Story

1. *What is Sara's school project about?*

   a) Physics
   b) Chemical reactions
   c) Biology

2. *What does Sara wear for safety during her experiment?*

   a) Apron
   b) Safety goggles
   c) Gloves

3. *What happens to the solution in the test tube during Sara's experiment?*

   a) It freezes
   b) It changes color and bubbles
   c) It becomes solid

4. *Who observes Sara conducting her experiment?*

   a) Her friends
   b) Her parents
   c) Her teacher

5. *What does Sara do with her observations?*

   a) Tells her friends
   b) Writes them down
   c) Ignores them

Correct Answers:

1. b) Chemical reactions
2. b) Safety goggles
3. b) It changes color and bubbles
4. c) Her teacher
5. b) Writes them down

- Chapter Thirty-Seven -
THE LIBRARY ADVENTURE

Das Bibliotheksabenteuer

Emily besucht die Bibliothek, um ein Buch für ihr Geschichtsprojekt zu finden. Als sie die Bücherregale durchsucht, entdeckt sie ein geheimnisvolles Buch ohne Titel. Neugierig öffnet sie es und findet eine Karte, die zu einem verborgenen Teil der Bibliothek führt.

Mit einem Gefühl des Abenteuers folgt Emily der Karte. Sie flüstert zu sich selbst, aufgeregt über das Geheimnis. Die Bibliothekarin beobachtet sie mit einem Lächeln, denn sie kennt die Geheimnisse der Bibliothek.

Schließlich findet Emily den verborgenen Bereich. Er ist gefüllt mit alten Büchern und Geschichten. Sie verbringt Stunden mit Lesen und Entdecken neuer Dinge. Sie leiht sich einige Bücher aus, begierig darauf, zu Hause mehr zu lernen.

Als sie die Bücher zurückgibt, dankt Emily der Bibliothekarin für das unglaubliche Abenteuer. Sie hat nicht nur Bücher gefunden, sondern auch eine Liebe zum Lesen und zum Erforschen des Unbekannten.

Vocabulary

Library	Bibliothek
Bookshelf	Bücherregal
Adventure	Abenteuer
Mystery	Geheimnis
Librarian	Bibliothekarin
Catalog	Katalog
Whisper	Flüstern
Discover	Entdecken
Title	Titel
Author	Autor
Chapter	Kapitel
Story	Geschichte
Borrow	Ausleihen
Return	Zurückgeben
Reading	Lesen

Questions About the Story

1. *What does Emily discover in the library?*

    a) A mysterious book
    b) A hidden door
    c) A secret map

2. *What does the mysterious book contain?*

    a) A spell
    b) A map to a hidden section
    c) A history of the library

3. *Who watches Emily with a knowing smile?*

    a) A friend
    b) A ghost
    c) The librarian

4. *What is Emily's main purpose for visiting the library?*

    a) To return a book
    b) To meet friends
    c) To find a book for her history project

5. *How does Emily feel when following the map?*

    a) Scared
    b) Excited
    c) Confused

Correct Answers:

1. a) A mysterious book
2. b) A map to a hidden section
3. c) The librarian
4. c) To find a book for her history project
5. b) Excited

- Chapter Thirty-Eight -
A HIKING TRIP

Eine Wandertour

Tom und Lisa beschließen, eine Wandertour in den Bergen zu unternehmen. Sie packen ihre Rucksäcke mit Wasser, einer Karte und einem Kompass. Aufgeregt, der Natur nahe zu sein, starten sie ihr Abenteuer früh am Morgen.

Sie folgen einem markierten Weg und gehen durch einen dichten Wald, lauschen den Geräuschen der um sie herum lebenden Tiere. Der Pfad ist steil, aber Tom und Lisa genießen jeden Schritt und spüren die frische Bergluft.

Auf halber Strecke machen sie Halt, um zu zelten. Sie schlagen ihr Zelt auf und genießen die atemberaubende Aussicht auf das Tal unten. Die Nacht ist friedlich, und sie schlafen unter den Sternen ein.

Am nächsten Tag erreichen sie den Gipfel. Die Aussicht von oben ist atemberaubend. Sie erkunden die Gegend, machen Fotos, um ihre Reise zu dokumentieren. Zufrieden beginnen sie ihren Abstieg und planen bereits ihre nächste Wanderung.

Vocabulary

Hike	Wandern
Trail	Weg
Backpack	Rucksack
Map	Karte
Compass	Kompass
Nature	Natur
Mountain	Berg
Forest	Wald
Camp	Zelten
View	Aussicht
Path	Pfad
Wildlife	Tierwelt
Tent	Zelt
Summit	Gipfel
Explore	Erkunden

Questions About the Story

1. *What do Tom and Lisa decide to do?*

   a) Have a picnic
   b) Go on a hiking trip
   c) Go fishing

2. *What do they pack in their backpacks?*

   a) Water, a map, and a compass
   b) Sunscreen and a beach towel
   c) A laptop and headphones

3. *Where do they decide to camp?*

   a) At the beach
   b) In a forest clearing
   c) Halfway up the mountain

4. *What is the view like from the summit?*

   a) Breathtaking
   b) Cloudy
   c) Foggy

5. *What do they do at the summit?*

   a) Start a fire
   b) Build a snowman
   c) Take photos

Correct Answers:

1. b) Go on a hiking trip
2. a) Water, a map, and a compass
3. c) Halfway up the mountain
4. a) Breathtaking
5. c) Take photos

- Chapter Thirty-Nine -
THE SCHOOL DANCE

Der Schulball

Die Turnhalle der Schule wird für den jährlichen Schulball umgestaltet. Bunte Lichter und Musik erfüllen den Raum und schaffen eine lebhafte Atmosphäre. Emma und ihre Freunde sind aufgeregt und tragen ihre besten Outfits.

Die Musik beginnt, und alle fangen an zu tanzen. Emma fühlt sich anfangs schüchtern, findet aber bald den Rhythmus und bewegt sich selbstbewusst. Sie lacht und genießt den Moment, spürt den Beat der Musik.

Jake, ein Freund aus der Klasse, bittet Emma zum Tanz. Gemeinsam gesellen sie sich zu den anderen auf der Tanzfläche und bewegen sich im Takt eines Lieblingsliedes. Der Raum ist erfüllt von Energie und Lachen, während die Schüler die Nacht genießen.

Als das letzte Lied spielt, versammeln sich Emma und ihre Freunde im Kreis, halten sich an den Händen und tanzen. Sie sind glücklich und dankbar für den spaßigen Abend. Der Schulball ist eine Erinnerung, die sie schätzen werden.

Vocabulary

Dance	Tanzen
Music	Musik
Friend	Freund
Dress	Kleid
Suit	Anzug
Gym	Turnhalle
Move	Bewegen
Beat	Beat
Partner	Partner
Fun	Spaß
Song	Lied
DJ	DJ
Step	Schritt
Laugh	Lachen
Enjoy	Genießen

Questions About the Story

1. *What did Tom and Lisa decide to do?*

    a) Go on a beach vacation
    b) Take a boat trip
    c) Go on a hiking trip in the mountains

2. *What did they bring with them for the hike?*

    a) Just a map
    b) Water, a map, and a compass
    c) Only their cellphones

3. *Where did they stop to camp?*

    a) At the summit
    b) Halfway up the mountain
    c) In the dense forest

4. *What was the atmosphere like during their hike?*

    a) Noisy and crowded
    b) Quiet and filled with the sounds of wildlife
    c) Extremely windy and uncomfortable

5. *What did they do at the summit?*

    a) Decided to camp there
    b) Took photos to remember their journey
    c) Called for help to descend

Correct Answers:

1. c) Go on a hiking trip in the mountains
2. b) Water, a map, and a compass
3. b) Halfway up the mountain
4. b) Quiet and filled with the sounds of wildlife
5. b) Took photos to remember their journey

- Chapter Forty -
AN UNEXPECTED JOURNEY

Eine unerwartete Reise

Mark erhält einen geheimnisvollen Brief mit einer Karte und einer Einladung zu einer unerwarteten Reise. Neugierig packt er seinen Rucksack und macht sich auf den Weg, gespannt darauf, was vor ihm liegt.

Der Karte folgend, reist Mark durch verschiedene Landschaften, jede schöner als die vorherige. Er trifft einen sachkundigen Führer, der Geschichten über die lokale Kultur und Sehenswürdigkeiten teilt.

Ihr Abenteuer führt sie durch antike Ruinen, über Flüsse und in lebhafte Städte. Unterwegs lernt und erlebt Mark Dinge, die er sich nie vorstellen konnte. Die Reise lehrt ihn den Wert der Erkundung und die Schönheit, das Unbekannte zu entdecken.

Als Mark nach Hause zurückkehrt, erkennt er, dass der wahre Schatz die Reise selbst und die Erinnerungen waren, die er gemacht hat. Er freut sich mit Aufregung und offenem Herzen auf sein nächstes Abenteuer.

Vocabulary

Journey	Reise
Surprise	Überraschung
Destination	Ziel
Travel	Reisen
Map	Karte
Discover	Entdecken
Adventure	Abenteuer
Guide	Führer
Explore	Erkunden
Route	Route
Vehicle	Fahrzeug
Backpack	Rucksack
Landmark	Wahrzeichen
Culture	Kultur
Experience	Erfahrung

Questions About the Story

1. *What does Mark receive that inspires him to start his journey?*

    a) A mysterious letter and a map
    b) A phone call from a friend
    c) A digital message

2. *What does Mark pack for his journey?*

    a) Just a camera and a notebook
    b) A backpack with water, a map, and a compass
    c) Only his phone and wallet

3. *Who does Mark meet that helps him during his journey?*

    a) A mysterious stranger
    b) A family member
    c) A knowledgeable guide

4. *What types of landscapes does Mark travel through?*

    a) Deserts and cities only
    b) Mountains and forests
    c) Ancient ruins, rivers, and vibrant cities

5. *What does Mark learn is the real treasure from his journey?*

    a) Gold and jewels
    b) The journey itself and the memories made
    c) A hidden artifact

Correct Answers:

1. a) A mysterious letter and a map
2. b) A backpack with water, a map, and a compass
3. c) A knowledgeable guide
4. c) Ancient ruins, rivers, and vibrant cities
5. b) The journey itself and the memories made

- Chapter Forty-One -
THE CULTURAL FESTIVAL

Das Kulturfestival

Der Stadtplatz ist lebendig mit dem jährlichen Kulturfestival. Bunte Stände säumen die Straßen, jeder repräsentiert unterschiedliche Kulturen mit Musik, Tanz und traditionellen Kostümen. Anna und Ben sind gespannt auf die Erkundung.

Sie beginnen mit einer Tanzvorführung, bei der Tänzer in lebhaften Kostümen sich im Rhythmus traditioneller Musik bewegen. Anna und Ben klatschen mit, gefesselt von der Energie und dem Können.

Als Nächstes schlendern sie durch die Essensstände und kosten Gerichte aus aller Welt. Die Aromen sind verlockend, und jeder Bissen ist eine Entdeckung neuer Geschmacksrichtungen.

Am Kunsthandwerksstand bewundern sie handgemachte Kunstwerke, die jeweils eine Geschichte von Erbe und Tradition erzählen. Sie sehen sich eine Parade von Darstellern an, wobei jede Gruppe stolz ihre Kultur präsentiert.

Das Festival ist eine Feier der Vielfalt und Einheit. Anna und Ben gehen mit einer tieferen Wertschätzung für die Kulturen der Welt, ihr Herz voller Musik und ihr Geist bereichert durch neues Wissen.

Vocabulary

Festival	*Festival*
Culture	*Kultur*
Dance	*Tanz*
Music	*Musik*
Tradition	*Tradition*
Costume	*Kostüm*
Food	*Essen*
Craft	*Handwerk*
Parade	*Parade*
Exhibit	*Ausstellung*
Celebration	*Feier*
Performance	*Vorführung*
Art	*Kunst*
Booth	*Stand*
Heritage	*Erbe*

Questions About the Story

1. *What prompted Tom and Lisa to pack for their adventure?*

   a) A hiking trip in the mountains
   b) A beach vacation
   c) A skiing holiday

2. *What did Tom and Lisa bring with them for the hike?*

   a) Sunscreen and a surfboard
   b) A map and a compass
   c) Ski equipment

3. *Where did Tom and Lisa decide to camp during their hike?*

   a) At the summit
   b) In a dense forest
   c) Near a beautiful valley

4. *What was the view like from the summit?*

   a) Cloudy and obscured
   b) Breathtaking
   c) No view, it was too dark

5. *What did Tom and Lisa do at the summit?*

   a) Set up their tent
   b) Took photos
   c) Went fishing

Correct Answers:

1. a) A hiking trip in the mountains
2. b) A map and a compass
3. c) Near a beautiful valley
4. b) Breathtaking
5. b) Took photos

- Chapter Forty-Two -
A DAY WITHOUT ELECTRICITY

Ein Tag ohne Strom

Eines Abends führt ein Stromausfall dazu, dass die Stadt in Dunkelheit versinkt. Emma und ihre Familie finden sich ohne Strom wieder. Sie zünden Kerzen an und versammeln sich im Wohnzimmer, eine Taschenlampe wirft Schatten an die Wände.

Die Stille ohne das übliche Summen der Elektronik ist ungewöhnlich, aber friedlich. Sie beschließen, bei Kerzenschein Brettspiele zu spielen, lachen und genießen die Gesellschaft des anderen auf eine Weise, wie sie es lange nicht getan haben.

Emma liest ein Buch im Licht einer Laterne, die Geschichte wird im flackernden Licht noch fesselnder. Draußen leuchten die Sterne heller ohne die Stadtbeleuchtung, und die Familie tritt hinaus, um den Nachthimmel zu betrachten, staunend über die Schönheit der Sterne.

Die Nacht ohne Strom bringt die Familie näher zusammen, erinnert sie an die Freude an einfachen Dingen und die Schönheit des Entschleunigens.

Vocabulary

Electricity	*Strom*
Candle	*Kerze*
Dark	*Dunkel*
Light	*Licht*
Battery	*Batterie*
Flashlight	*Taschenlampe*
Quiet	*Ruhe*
Read	*Lesen*
Board game	*Brettspiel*
Night	*Nacht*
Family	*Familie*
Talk	*Sprechen*
Fire	*Feuer*
Lantern	*Laterne*
Stars	*Sterne*

Questions About the Story

1. *What event leads to the family spending time together without electricity?*

    a) A city-wide celebration
    b) A power outage
    c) A decision to unplug for the day

2. *What do Emma and her family use for light during the power outage?*

    a) Electric lamps
    b) Candles and a flashlight
    c) The light from their phones

3. *How does the family spend their time during the power outage?*

    a) Watching television
    b) Playing board games
    c) Sleeping early

4. *What does Emma do by the light of a lantern?*

    a) Cooks dinner
    b) Reads a book
    c) Plays a musical instrument

5. *What natural phenomenon is more visible due to the power outage?*

    a) Rainbows
    b) The stars
    c) Northern lights

Correct Answers:

1. b) A power outage
2. b) Candles and a flashlight
3. b) Playing board games
4. b) Reads a book
5. b) The stars

- Chapter Forty-Three -
THE BIG GAME

Das große Spiel

Das örtliche Fußballteam hat es ins Finale geschafft, und die ganze Stadt ist voller Aufregung. Heute ist das große Spiel, und alle versammeln sich auf dem Spielfeld, tragen die Farben ihres Teams und sind bereit, anzufeuern.

Tom, der Star des Teams, spürt den Erwartungsdruck, ist aber entschlossen zu gewinnen. Der Trainer hält eine motivierende Rede, die das Team an ihre harte Arbeit und Hingabe erinnert.

Als das Spiel beginnt, jubelt die Menge laut. Der Wettbewerb ist hart, aber Tom gelingt es, in den letzten Minuten das entscheidende Tor zu schießen. Das Stadion bricht in Freude aus, als das Team ihren Sieg feiert.

Nach dem Spiel dankt das Team ihren Fans für ihre Unterstützung. Das große Spiel war nicht nur ein Sieg für das Team, sondern auch eine Feier des Gemeinschaftsgeistes und der Teamarbeit.

Vocabulary

Game	*Spiel*
Team	*Team*
Score	*Punkten*
Win	*Gewinnen*
Lose	*Verlieren*
Player	*Spieler*
Coach	*Trainer*
Field	*Spielfeld*
Cheer	*Anfeuern*
Uniform	*Uniform*
Ball	*Ball*
Goal	*Tor*
Match	*Match*
Referee	*Schiedsrichter*
Competition	*Wettbewerb*

Questions About the Story

1. *What event is the town excited about?*

    a) A local festival
    b) The championship football game
    c) A concert

2. *Who is the star player of the team?*

    a) The coach
    b) Tom
    c) The goalkeeper

3. *What did the coach do before the game started?*

    a) Gave a motivational speech
    b) Scored a goal
    c) Left the stadium

4. *How did the crowd react as the game started?*

    a) They were silent
    b) They booed
    c) They cheered loudly

5. *What was the outcome of the game?*

    a) The team lost
    b) The team won
    c) The game was canceled

Correct Answers:

1. b) The championship football game
2. b) Tom
3. a) Gave a motivational speech
4. c) They cheered loudly
5. b) The team won

- Chapter Forty-Four -
A MYSTERY GUEST

Ein geheimnisvoller Gast

Auf Annas jährlicher Party gibt es Gerüchte über einen geheimnisvollen Gast. Anna schickt Einladungen mit einem Hinweis: „Dieses Jahr wird ein Überraschungsgast unseren Abend unvergesslich machen." Alle sind gespannt und rätseln, wer es sein könnte.

Am Abend der Party kommen die Gäste an, voller Spekulationen und Getuschel über den geheimnisvollen Gast. Das Haus ist lebendig, erfüllt von Lachen und Musik. Anna genießt die Aufregung, hält das Geheimnis jedoch gut versteckt.

Mitten in der Party versammelt Anna alle. „Es ist Zeit, unseren geheimnisvollen Gast zu enthüllen!" kündigt sie an. Der Raum wird still vor Erwartung. Dann tritt aus einem anderen Raum der geheimnisvolle Gast hervor – es ist ein berühmter lokaler Musiker, ein Freund von Anna, der im Ausland auf Tour war.

Die Gäste sind begeistert, brechen in Applaus und Jubel aus. Der Musiker spielt einige Lieder, was den Abend wirklich unvergesslich macht. Der geheimnisvolle Gast war das Highlight der Party, und alle danken Anna für diese wunderbare Überraschung.

Vocabulary

Guest	Gast
Mystery	Geheimnis
Invite	Einladen
Party	Party
Surprise	Überraschung
Guess	Raten
Reveal	Enthüllen
Host	Gastgeber
Evening	Abend
Secret	Geheimnis
Clue	Hinweis
Discover	Entdecken
Whisper	Flüstern
Excitement	Aufregung
Unveil	Enthüllen

Questions About the Story

1. *What was the occasion at Anna's house?*

   a) A birthday party
   b) An annual party
   c) A wedding celebration

2. *What clue did Anna provide about the surprise guest in the invites?*

   a) "A famous actor will join us."
   b) "This year, a surprise guest will make our evening
      unforgettable."
   c) "Guess who's coming to dinner."

3. *How did the guests react to the anticipation of the mystery guest?*

   a) They were indifferent
   b) They were excited and guessing
   c) They were confused

4. *Who was the mystery guest?*

   a) A famous author
   b) A local teacher
   c) A famous local musician

5. *What did the mystery guest do at the party?*

   a) Gave a speech
   b) Performed a few songs
   c) Cooked for the guests

Correct Answers:

1. b) An annual party
2. b) "This year, a surprise guest will make our evening unforgettable."
3. b) They were excited and guessing
4. c) A famous local musician
5. b) Performed a few songs

- Chapter Forty-Five -
THE CHARITY EVENT

Die Wohltätigkeitsveranstaltung

Das Gemeindezentrum organisiert eine Wohltätigkeitsveranstaltung zur Unterstützung einer lokalen Ursache. Jeder ist eingeladen teilzunehmen, zu spenden und zu helfen, einen Unterschied zu machen. Die Veranstaltung umfasst eine Auktion, bei der von Gemeindemitgliedern gespendete Gegenstände versteigert werden.

Sarah arbeitet freiwillig bei der Veranstaltung, hilft bei der Organisation der Auktionsartikel und begrüßt die Gäste. Sie ist bewegt von der Großzügigkeit der Menschen, die zusammenkommen, um die Ursache zu unterstützen.

Als die Auktion beginnt, füllt sich das Gemeindezentrum mit eifrigen Bietern. Jeder versteigerte Artikel bringt mehr Geld für die Ursache ein, und Sarah empfindet Stolz und Freude über das Engagement ihrer Gemeinschaft.

Die Veranstaltung ist ein Erfolg, es werden bedeutende Mittel aufgebracht. Die Unterstützung und Großzügigkeit der Gemeinschaft übertrifft die Erwartungen, und die Organisatoren danken allen für ihre Beiträge und den Geist des Gebens.

Vocabulary

Charity	*Wohltätigkeit*
Event	*Veranstaltung*
Donate	*Spenden*
Fundraise	*Geld sammeln*
Volunteer	*Freiwilliger*
Help	*Helfen*
Cause	*Ursache*
Support	*Unterstützen*
Money	*Geld*
Auction	*Auktion*
Community	*Gemeinde*
Generosity	*Großzügigkeit*
Benefit	*Nutzen*
Organize	*Organisieren*
Contribution	*Beitrag*

Questions About the Story

1. *What type of event does the community center organize?*

    a) A music concert
    b) A charity event
    c) A sports tournament

2. *What is included in the charity event?*

    a) A fashion show
    b) An auction
    c) A cooking competition

3. *What role does Sarah play at the event?*

    a) Auctioneer
    b) Performer
    c) Volunteer

4. *What does Sarah feel about the community's effort?*

    a) Disappointed
    b) Indifferent
    c) Proud and joyful

5. *What does the auction contribute to?*

    a) Raising funds for a local cause
    b) Celebrating the community's anniversary
    c) Funding the community center's renovation

Correct Answers:

1. b) A charity event
2. b) An auction
3. c) Volunteer
4. c) Proud and joyful
5. a) Raising funds for a local cause

- Chapter Forty-Six -
LEARNING TO SKATE

Schlittschuhlaufen lernen

Emily beschließt, Schlittschuhlaufen zu lernen, und meldet sich für Unterricht in der örtlichen Eisbahn an. Am ersten Tag ist sie sowohl nervös als auch aufgeregt. Sie zieht ihre Schlittschuhe an, betritt das Eis und fühlt sich sofort unsicher.

Ihr Trainer, Herr Jones, ermutigt sie, weiterzumachen. „Balance ist der Schlüssel", sagt er. Emily übt das Gleiten und Drehen und fühlt sich nach und nach sicherer auf dem Eis. Sie fällt ein paar Mal, lacht aber darüber und steht wieder auf.

Mit jeder Stunde verbessern sich Emilys Fähigkeiten. Sie lernt, schneller und mit mehr Agilität zu laufen. Ihre Angst zu fallen nimmt ab, da sie sich immer wohler auf dem Eis fühlt.

Am Ende der Saison kann Emily anmutig um die Eisbahn laufen. Sie ist dankbar für die Geduld und Anleitung von Herrn Jones. Schlittschuhlaufen zu lernen hat ihr nicht nur das Gleichgewicht auf dem Eis beigebracht, sondern auch Ausdauer und die Überwindung von Ängsten.

Vocabulary

Skate	*Schlittschuh laufen*
Ice	*Eis*
Rink	*Eisbahn*
Balance	*Balance*
Fall	*Fallen*
Helmet	*Helm*
Glide	*Gleiten*
Coach	*Trainer*
Practice	*Üben*
Boots	*Stiefel*
Turn	*Drehen*
Learn	*Lernen*
Speed	*Geschwindigkeit*
Safety	*Sicherheit*
Lesson	*Unterricht*

Questions About the Story

1. *Why did Emily decide to take ice skating lessons?*

   a) She wanted to become a professional skater
   b) She was looking for a new hobby
   c) She wanted to learn something challenging

2. *How did Emily feel when she first stepped onto the ice?*

   a) Confident and ready
   b) Nervous and excited
   c) Disappointed and scared

3. *What key advice did Mr. Jones give to Emily?*

   a) Speed is everything
   b) Balance is key
   c) Practice makes perfect

4. *What was Emily's reaction to falling on the ice?*

   a) She gave up immediately
   b) She cried and felt embarrassed
   c) She laughed it off and got back up

5. *How did Emily's skills change over the course of her lessons?*

   a) They deteriorated due to lack of practice
   b) They slightly improved but not significantly
   c) She learned to skate faster and with more agility

Correct Answers:

1. c) She wanted to learn something challenging
2. b) Nervous and excited
3. b) Balance is key
4. c) She laughed it off and got back up
5. c) She learned to skate faster and with more agility

- Chapter Forty-Seven -
A HISTORICAL TOUR

Eine historische Tour

Tom und Sara beschließen, an einer historischen Tour durch ihre Stadt teilzunehmen. Sie treffen ihren Führer, Herrn Lee, am Eingang des Museums. „Heute werden wir die reiche Geschichte unserer Stadt erkunden", kündigt Herr Lee an.

Ihre erste Station ist ein großes Schloss aus dem 12. Jahrhundert. „Dieses Schloss war Zeuge vieler wichtiger Ereignisse", erklärt Herr Lee. Tom und Sara sind fasziniert von der alten Architektur und den Geschichten aus der Vergangenheit.

Weiter geht es zu den Ruinen eines alten Denkmals. Herr Lee erzählt Geschichten über die Menschen, die einst dort lebten. Tom und Sara fühlen sich, als würden sie durch die Zeit reisen.

Die Tour endet im Museum, wo sie Artefakte und Ausstellungen über die Kultur und das Erbe der Stadt sehen. Sie erfahren mehr über die alten Werkzeuge, Kleidung und Kunst, die die Geschichte ihrer Stadt geprägt haben.

Tom und Sara verlassen die Tour erleuchtet und dankbar für die Chance, die Vergangenheit ihrer Stadt zu entdecken. Sie planen, gemeinsam weitere historische Orte zu erkunden.

Vocabulary

Historical	*Historisch*
Tour	*Tour*
Monument	*Denkmal*
Guide	*Führer*
Century	*Jahrhundert*
Castle	*Schloss*
Museum	*Museum*
Artifact	*Artefakt*
Explore	*Erkunden*
Ruins	*Ruinen*
Discover	*Entdecken*
Ancient	*Antik*
Exhibition	*Ausstellung*
Culture	*Kultur*
Heritage	*Erbe*

Questions About the Story

1. Who leads the historical tour Tom and Sara join?

    a) Mr. Lee
    b) A museum curator
    c) A history professor

2. What is the first historical site Tom and Sara visit on their tour?

    a) A medieval village
    b) An ancient monument
    c) A grand castle from the 12th century

3. What do Tom and Sara feel as they explore the castle?

    a) Boredom
    b) Confusion
    c) Fascination and wonder

4. Where does the tour end?

    a) At the city hall
    b) Back at the museum
    c) In the city square

5. What do Tom and Sara learn about at the museum?

    a) Modern art
    b) The city's future plans
    c) The city's culture and heritage

Correct Answers:

1. a) Mr. Lee
2. c) A grand castle from the 12th century
3. c) Fascination and wonder
4. b) Back at the museum
5. c) The city's culture and heritage

- Chapter Forty-Eight -
THE BAKE SALE

Der Kuchenverkauf

Lisa und ihre Freunde organisieren an ihrer Schule einen Kuchenverkauf, um Geld für ein örtliches Tierheim zu sammeln. Sie verbringen den ganzen Tag davor mit Backen von Kuchen, Keksen und Torten.

Am Tag des Verkaufs richtet Lisa einen Tisch mit all den köstlichen Leckereien ein. „Alles riecht so gut", denkt sie und hofft, dass viele Leute ihre Backwaren kaufen werden.

Der Verkauf ist ein Erfolg! Die Leute lieben die süßen Kekse und die fluffigen Kuchen. Lisa und ihre Freunde mischen verschiedene Zutaten, um einzigartige Geschmacksrichtungen zu kreieren, welche die Favoriten werden.

Am Ende des Tages ist fast alles ausverkauft. Lisa zählt das Geld und ist begeistert zu sehen, wie viel sie für das Tierheim gesammelt haben. „Diese Spendensammlung war eine großartige Idee", sagt sie.

Der Kuchenverkauf hilft nicht nur dem Tierheim, sondern bringt auch die Gemeinschaft für eine süße Sache zusammen.

Vocabulary

Bake	*Backen*
Sale	*Verkauf*
Cake	*Kuchen*
Cookie	*Keks*
Oven	*Ofen*
Dough	*Teig*
Mix	*Mischen*
Recipe	*Rezept*
Ingredient	*Zutat*
Sweet	*Süß*
Pie	*Torte*
Fundraiser	*Spendensammlung*
Delicious	*Köstlich*
Sugar	*Zucker*
Flour	*Mehl*

Questions About the Story

1. *What was the purpose of the bake sale organized by Lisa and her friends?*

    a) To fund a school trip
    b) To support a local animal shelter
    c) To buy new sports equipment for the school

2. *What items did Lisa and her friends bake for the sale?*

    a) Cakes, cookies, and pies
    b) Sandwiches and salads
    c) Vegan and gluten-free snacks

3. *What was Lisa's hope for the bake sale?*

    a) To sell out everything by noon
    b) To raise enough money for a new animal shelter
    c) That many people would buy their baked goods

4. *How did the community respond to the bake sale?*

    a) They ignored the sale
    b) They complained about the prices
    c) They loved the sweet cookies and the fluffy cakes

5. *What unique approach did Lisa and her friends take for their baked goods?*

    a) Using family recipes
    b) Mixing different ingredients to create unique flavors
    c) Baking everything with organic ingredients

Correct Answers:

1. b) To support a local animal shelter
2. a) Cakes, cookies, and pies
3. c) That many people would buy their baked goods
4. c) They loved the sweet cookies and the fluffy cakes
5. b) Mixing different ingredients to create unique flavors

- Chapter Forty-Nine -
THE TALENT SHOW

Die Talentshow

Im lokalen Gemeindezentrum findet eine Talentshow statt, bei der jeder auftreten darf. Emma beschließt zu singen, und ihr Bruder Jake wird einen Zaubertrick vorführen.

Die Bühne ist bereit, und das Publikum ist gespannt auf die Auftritte. Emma ist nervös, aber aufgeregt. Als sie dran ist, singt sie wunderschön, und das Publikum applaudiert laut.

Jake folgt mit seinen Zaubertricks, lässt einen Hasen verschwinden und wieder erscheinen. Die Zuschauer sind verblüfft und spenden ihm großen Applaus.

Die Jury tut sich schwer mit der Entscheidung, aber am Ende vergeben sie Preise an die herausragendsten Talente. Emma und Jake gewinnen nicht, sind aber glücklich, aufgetreten zu sein.

Die Talentshow bringt die Gemeinschaft zusammen und feiert die vielfältigen Talente unter ihnen. Emma und Jake freuen sich darauf, nächstes Jahr wieder teilzunehmen.

Vocabulary

Talent	*Talent*
Show	*Show*
Perform	*Auftreten*
Stage	*Bühne*
Audience	*Publikum*
Judge	*Juror*
Act	*Nummer*
Sing	*Singen*
Dance	*Tanzen*
Magic	*Zauberei*
Award	*Preis*
Applause	*Applaus*
Contestant	*Teilnehmer*
Juggle	*Jonglieren*
Performer	*Darsteller*

Questions About the Story

1. *What event do Emma and Jake participate in?*

   a) A bake sale
   b) A talent show
   c) A school play

2. *What talent does Emma showcase at the talent show?*

   a) Dancing
   b) Singing
   c) Magic tricks

3. *What does Jake perform in the talent show?*

   a) A dance
   b) A song
   c) A magic act

4. *How does the audience react to Emma's performance?*

   a) They leave the room
   b) They boo
   c) They applaud loudly

5. *What magic trick does Jake perform?*

   a) Pulling a hat out of a rabbit
   b) Making a rabbit disappear and reappear
   c) Levitating

Correct Answers:

1. b) A talent show
2. b) Singing
3. c) A magic act
4. c) They applaud loudly
5. b) Making a rabbit disappear and reappear

- Chapter Fifty -
A DAY WITH GRANDPARENTS

Ein Tag mit den Großeltern

Anna besucht ihre Großeltern für einen Tag. Sie leben in einem Haus mit einem großen Garten. „Wir haben einen besonderen Tag geplant", sagt ihre Großmutter mit einem Lächeln.

Zuerst backen sie zusammen Kekse. Annas Großmutter bringt ihr bei, wie man den Teig mischt. „Backen ist eine Tradition in unserer Familie", erklärt sie. Sie genießen die warmen Kekse zum Mittagessen.

Nach dem Mittagessen gehen sie in den Garten. Ihr Großvater zeigt Anna, wie man Samen pflanzt. „Gärten sind wie Familien; sie wachsen mit Liebe und Pflege", sagt er.

Sie verbringen den Nachmittag damit, alte Familienfotos anzuschauen. „Diese Erinnerungen sind kostbar", sagt ihre Großmutter und umarmt Anna.

Bevor sie geht, umarmt Anna ihre Großeltern. „Heute war wunderbar. Danke, dass ihr mir so viel beigebracht habt", sagt sie. Sie lächeln, glücklich, ihre Weisheit und Liebe geteilt zu haben.

Vocabulary

Grandparents	*Großeltern*
Story	*Geschichte*
Bake	*Backen*
Garden	*Garten*
Teach	*Lehren*
Memory	*Erinnerung*
Love	*Liebe*
Old	*Alt*
Wisdom	*Weisheit*
Photo	*Foto*
Lunch	*Mittagessen*
Hug	*Umarmung*
Family	*Familie*
Tradition	*Tradition*
Smile	*Lächeln*

Questions About the Story

1. *What activity did Anna and her grandparents start with?*

    a) Planting seeds
    b) Baking cookies
    c) Looking at old family photos

2. *What metaphor did Anna's grandpa use to describe gardens?*

    a) Gardens need sunlight to grow
    b) Gardens are like families; they grow with love and care
    c) Gardens are full of surprises

3. *What did Anna and her grandparents enjoy after baking?*

    a) They went for a walk in the garden
    b) They had lunch and enjoyed the warm cookies
    c) They started planting seeds immediately

4. *What did Anna learn from her grandparents?*

    a) How to bake cookies and plant seeds
    b) The history of their family
    c) Both A and B

5. *What was the special day planned by Anna's grandparents?*

    a) A baking day
    b) A gardening day
    c) A day full of family activities

Correct Answers:

1. b) Baking cookies
2. b) Gardens are like families; they grow with love and care
3. b) They had lunch and enjoyed the warm cookies
4. c) Both A and B
5. c) A day full of family activities

- Chapter Fifty-One -
THE PUZZLE CHALLENGE

Die Rätselherausforderung

In der Schule kündigt Frau Clark eine Rätselherausforderung an. „Das wird eure Logik und Teamarbeit auf die Probe stellen", sagt sie. Die Klasse ist aufgeregt.

Jedes Team erhält ein Puzzle mit vielen Teilen. „Lasst uns sorgfältig denken und zusammenarbeiten", sagt Leo, der Teamleiter. Sie beginnen, das Puzzle zu lösen und versuchen, die Teile zusammenzufügen.

Auf halbem Weg kommen sie ins Stocken. „Wir müssen das fehlende Teil finden", sagt Mia und schaut sich um. Nach einem Moment des Nachdenkens finden sie den Hinweis, der sie zur Lösung führt.

Am Ende ist ihr Team das erste, das das Puzzle vervollständigt. „Großartige Arbeit, alle zusammen! Eure Teamarbeit und Logik waren beeindruckend", lobt Frau Clark sie.

Die Rätselherausforderung war nicht nur ein Spiel, sondern auch eine Lektion in Zusammenarbeit und Problemlösung.

Vocabulary

Puzzle	*Puzzle*
Challenge	*Herausforderung*
Solve	*Lösen*
Piece	*Teil*
Think	*Denken*
Brain	*Gehirn*
Game	*Spiel*
Clue	*Hinweis*
Mystery	*Geheimnis*
Team	*Team*
Logic	*Logik*
Answer	*Antwort*
Question	*Frage*
Riddle	*Rätsel*
Compete	*Wettstreiten*

Questions About the Story

1. *Who announces the puzzle challenge in school?*

   a) Mr. Lee
   b) Mrs. Clark
   c) Mia

2. *What is Leo's role in the team?*

   a) The team leader
   b) The class president
   c) The puzzle master

3. *What does Mia say when the team gets stuck?*

   a) "Let's give up."
   b) "We need to find the missing piece."
   c) "This is too hard."

4. *What was the key to completing the puzzle?*

   a) Cheating
   b) Asking the teacher for help
   c) Finding a missing piece

5. *How did Mrs. Clark praise the team?*

   a) "Your teamwork and logic were impressive."
   b) "You should have done better."
   c) "You were the slowest."

Correct Answers:

1. b) Mrs. Clark
2. a) The team leader
3. b) "We need to find the missing piece."
4. c) Finding a missing piece
5. a) "Your teamwork and logic were impressive."

- Chapter Fifty-Two -
A CAMPING MYSTERY

Ein Camping-Geheimnis

Während eines Campingausflugs hören Mike und seine Freunde nachts seltsame Geräusche. „Hast du das gehört?", fragt Mike, während sie um das Lagerfeuer sitzen.

Neugierig beschließen sie, mit ihren Taschenlampen nachzuforschen. „Es klingt, als käme es aus dieser Richtung", sagt Sara und zeigt auf den dunklen Wald.

Als sie dem Geräusch folgen, finden sie Spuren am Boden. „Das sehen aus wie Tierpfoten", bemerkt Mike. Das Rätsel vertieft sich.

Plötzlich sehen sie einen Schatten sich bewegen. Sie bereiten sich auf etwas Erschreckendes vor, aber entdecken nur einen verirrten Hund. „Er muss die Geräusche gemacht haben", sagt Sara erleichtert.

Sie kehren zu ihrem Zelt zurück und bringen den Hund mit. „Dieser Campingausflug wurde zu einem unerwarteten Abenteuer", sagt Mike, während sie alle lachen und den Rest ihrer Nacht sicher am Feuer genießen.

Vocabulary

Camping	*Camping*
Mystery	*Geheimnis*
Tent	*Zelt*
Night	*Nacht*
Forest	*Wald*
Flashlight	*Taschenlampe*
Noise	*Geräusch*
Fire	*Feuer*
Scary	*Erschreckend*
Track	*Spur*
Dark	*Dunkel*
Campfire	*Lagerfeuer*
Investigate	*Untersuchen*
Shadow	*Schatten*
Scream	*Schrei*

Questions About the Story

1. *What do Mike and his friends hear at night during their camping trip?*

   a) Strange noises
   b) Music
   c) Thunder

2. *What do Mike and his friends use to investigate the strange noises?*

   a) Flashlights
   b) Mobile phones
   c) Lanterns

3. *Where do the strange noises seem to be coming from?*

   a) The lake
   b) Another campsite
   c) The dark forest

4. *What do Mike and his friends find on the ground that adds to the mystery?*

   a) A map
   b) Animal tracks
   c) A lost item

5. *What do Mike and his friends discover as the source of the noises?*

   a) A ghost
   b) A lost dog
   c) An owl

Correct Answers:

1. a) Strange noises
2. a) Flashlights
3. c) The dark forest
4. b) Animal tracks
5. b) A lost dog

- Chapter Fifty-Three -
DISCOVERING A NEW HOBBY

Ein neues Hobby entdecken

Emma langweilte sich mit ihrer üblichen Wochenendroutine. Eines Tages beschloss sie, etwas Neues zu erkunden, um ihr Interesse zu wecken. „Ich brauche ein Hobby", dachte sie sich.

Sie begann mit dem Malen und versuchte, einfache Kunstwerke zu schaffen. Obwohl ihre ersten Versuche nicht perfekt waren, genoss sie den Prozess sehr. „Das macht Spaß", erkannte Emma, als sie Farben mischte und sah, wie ihre Ideen auf der Leinwand zum Leben erwachten.

Als Nächstes versuchte Emma sich im Basteln. Sie fand Freude daran, kleine dekorative Gegenstände für ihr Zuhause zu machen. Jedes fertige Kunstwerk gab ihr ein Gefühl der Vollendung.

Ihre Neugier wuchs und führte sie zur Fotografie. Emma verbrachte Stunden damit, die Schönheit der Natur mit ihrer Kamera einzufangen. „Es gibt so viel zu sehen und zu lernen", staunte sie, als sie ihre Fotos durchsah.

Emmas Reise in die Welt der neuen Hobbys brachte ihr nicht nur Aufregung, sondern auch neue Fähigkeiten und eine tiefere Wertschätzung für Kreativität. „Ich bin froh, dass ich beschlossen habe, etwas anderes auszuprobieren", reflektierte sie und plante ihr nächstes Hobbyabenteuer.

Vocabulary

Hobby	*Hobby*
Discover	*Entdecken*
Interest	*Interesse*
Learn	*Lernen*
Practice	*Üben*
Skill	*Fähigkeit*
Fun	*Spaß*
Activity	*Aktivität*
Craft	*Basteln*
Paint	*Malen*
Collection	*Sammlung*
Music	*Musik*
Book	*Buch*
Photography	*Fotografie*
Drawing	*Zeichnen*

Questions About the Story

1. *What motivates Emma to find a new hobby?*

    a) She felt bored with her usual weekend routine
    b) She wanted to join her friends
    c) She needed to complete a school project

2. *Which of the following is NOT a hobby that Emma tried?*

    a) Painting
    b) Photography
    c) Gardening

3. *How does Emma feel about her first attempts at painting?*

    a) Disappointed
    b) Indifferent
    c) Enjoyed the process immensely

4. *What realization does Emma have while engaging in her new hobbies?*

    a) She prefers outdoor activities
    b) She enjoys the process of learning and creating
    c) She wants to become a professional artist

5. *Which hobby did Emma explore last?*

    a) Painting
    b) Crafting
    c) Photography

Correct Answers:

1. a) She felt bored with her usual weekend routine
2. c) Gardening
3. c) Enjoyed the process immensely
4. b) She enjoys the process of learning and creating
5. c) Photography

- Chapter Fifty-Four -
THE FRIENDLY COMPETITION

Der freundliche Wettbewerb

In der Schule wird der jährliche Sporttag mit viel Aufregung und freundlichem Wettbewerb erwartet. Alex und Jamie, zwei gute Freunde, melden sich für das Staffellauf an.

„Möge das beste Team gewinnen", sagten sie zueinander mit einem Lächeln und gaben sich vor dem Rennen die Hand. Ihre Teams waren bereit, und die Atmosphäre war elektrisierend vor Erwartung.

Als das Rennen begann, erfüllten Jubelrufe die Luft. Alex und Jamie liefen mit aller Kraft und übergaben den Staffelstab reibungslos an ihre Teamkollegen. Der Wettbewerb war knapp, aber am Ende gewann Alex' Team mit einem Bruchteil einer Sekunde.

Trotz der Niederlage war Jamie nicht verärgert. „Das war ein großartiges Rennen", gratulierte Jamie Alex, „Dein Team war heute fantastisch!"

Beide stimmten zu, dass Gewinnen Spaß macht, aber die Teilnahme und das Genießen des Spiels mit Freunden war das, was wirklich zählte. Ihre Freundschaft blieb stark, verbunden durch den Geist des gesunden Wettbewerbs.

Vocabulary

Competition	*Wettbewerb*
Friendly	*Freundlich*
Win	*Gewinnen*
Lose	*Verlieren*
Prize	*Preis*
Race	*Rennen*
Team	*Team*
Sport	*Sport*
Play	*Spielen*
Challenge	*Herausforderung*
Score	*Punkten*
Match	*Spiel*
Fun	*Spaß*
Opponent	*Gegner*
Cheer	*Anfeuern*

Questions About the Story

1. *What event brings Alex and Jamie to compete?*

    a) A science fair
    b) A relay race
    c) A chess tournament

2. *What was Alex and Jamie's attitude before the race?*

    a) Competitive
    b) Indifferent
    c) Supportive

3. *How did Alex and Jamie prepare for the race?*

    a) By studying
    b) By training
    c) By strategizing with their team

4. *What was the outcome of the relay race?*

    a) Jamie's team won
    b) Alex's team won
    c) It was a tie

5. *How did Jamie react to losing the race?*

    a) With disappointment
    b) With joy
    c) With sportsmanship

Correct Answers:

1. b) A relay race
2. c) Supportive
3. c) By strategizing with their team
4. b) Alex's team won
5. c) With sportsmanship

- Chapter Fifty-Five -
A VISIT TO THE GRAND CANYON

Ein Besuch im Grand Canyon

Lucas hatte schon immer davon geträumt, den Grand Canyon zu sehen. Eines Sommers machte er schließlich die Reise. „Das wird ein Abenteuer", dachte er, während er seinen Rucksack packte.

Als er am Rand des Canyons stand, war Lucas von der weiten Landschaft vor ihm überwältigt. Der Blick auf den tiefen Canyon mit seinen Schichten aus farbigem Gestein raubte ihm den Atem. „Es ist schöner, als ich es mir vorgestellt habe", flüsterte er sich zu.

Er verbrachte den Tag mit Wandern auf den Pfaden, staunte über die atemberaubenden Aussichten und die ruhige Schönheit der Natur. Lucas machte viele Fotos und versuchte, die Großartigkeit des Canyons einzufangen.

Bei Sonnenaufgang beobachtete er, wie der Canyon langsam durch das Morgenlicht erleuchtet wurde und eine atemberaubende Szene entstand. „Dieser Moment macht die ganze Reise wert", fühlte Lucas eine tiefe Verbindung zur Natur.

Sein Besuch im Grand Canyon war nicht nur ein Abhaken auf seiner Liste, sondern ein unvergessliches Erlebnis, das seine Wertschätzung für die natürliche Welt vertiefte.

Vocabulary

Canyon	Canyon
Grand	Groß
Nature	Natur
Hike	Wandern
View	Aussicht
Rock	Felsen
River	Fluss
Park	Park
Explore	Erforschen
Trail	Pfad
Landscape	Landschaft
Adventure	Abenteuer
Guide	Führer
Cliff	Klippe
Sunrise	Sonnenaufgang

Questions About the Story

1. *What inspired Lucas to make the trip?*

   a) A documentary
   b) A friend's suggestion
   c) A lifelong dream

2. *What was Lucas's reaction upon seeing the Grand Canyon?*

   a) He was slightly disappointed
   b) He was in awe
   c) He was indifferent

3. *What did Lucas do to try and capture the beauty of the Grand Canyon?*

   a) He wrote a poem
   b) He took many photos
   c) He painted a picture

4. *What time of day did Lucas find most breathtaking at the Grand Canyon?*

   a) Sunset
   b) Midday
   c) Sunrise

5. *How did Lucas feel about his trip to the Grand Canyon?*

   a) It was just another trip
   b) It was a disappointment
   c) It was a memorable experience

Correct Answers:

1. c) A lifelong dream
2. b) He was in awe
3. b) He took many photos
4. c) Sunrise
5. c) It was a memorable experience

- Chapter Fifty-Six -
THE HOMEMADE GIFT

Das selbstgemachte Geschenk

Für Annas Geburtstag beschloss ihre Freundin Maria, ein selbstgemachtes Geschenk zu machen. Maria dachte: „Ich möchte etwas Besonderes für Anna kreieren."

Maria liebte es zu basteln, also entschied sie sich, eine kleine Kiste zu bemalen und ein kleines Täschchen zu nähen. Sie strickte einen bunten Schal und entwarf ihn mit Anna im Sinn. „Anna wird diese lieben", lächelte Maria und stellte sich die Überraschung ihrer Freundin vor.

Nachdem sie die Handarbeiten fertiggestellt hatte, verpackte Maria die Geschenke sorgfältig. Sie verwendete ein helles Band, um das Paket zu binden und fügte eine handgemachte Karte hinzu, auf der sie schrieb: „Mit Liebe und Bedachtsamkeit."

Als Anna ihr Geschenk öffnete, leuchteten ihre Augen vor Freude auf. „Das ist so besonders! Danke, Maria", rief sie aus und umarmte ihre Freundin. Marias durchdachtes selbstgemachtes Geschenk machte Annas Geburtstag unvergesslich.

Vocabulary

Gift	*Geschenk*
Homemade	*Selbstgemacht*
Craft	*Basteln*
Surprise	*Überraschung*
Create	*Kreieren*
Paint	*Malen*
Sew	*Nähen*
Knit	*Stricken*
Design	*Entwerfen*
Special	*Besonders*
Card	*Karte*
Wrap	*Einpacken*
Ribbon	*Band*
Love	*Liebe*
Thoughtful	*Bedachtsam*

Questions About the Story

1. *What occasion is being celebrated in the story?*

   a) Maria's birthday
   b) Anna's birthday
   c) A holiday

2. *What type of gift does Maria decide to give Anna?*

   a) Store-bought jewelry
   b) Homemade crafts
   c) A book

3. *Which of the following items did Maria NOT craft for Anna?*

   a) A painted box
   b) A sewn pouch
   c) A ceramic vase

4. *How did Maria wrap the gift?*

   a) In a plain box
   b) With newspaper
   c) With bright ribbon and a handmade card

5. *What was Maria's intention behind creating the gift?*

   a) To save money
   b) To create something special for Anna
   c) Because she forgot to buy a gift

Correct Answers:

1. b) Anna's birthday
2. b) Homemade crafts
3. c) A ceramic vase
4. c) With bright ribbon and a handmade card
5. b) To create something special for Anna

- Chapter Fifty-Seven -
A SPECIAL DAY OUT

Ein besonderer Tag draußen

Liam und seine Familie beschließen, einen Tag im Vergnügungspark zu verbringen. „Das wird so viel Spaß machen!", ruft Liam aus und hält sein Ticket fest.

Ihre erste Station ist die Achterbahn. Liam fühlt eine Mischung aus Aufregung und Nervosität, während sie anstehen. „Los geht's!", schreit er, als die Achterbahn losrast.

Den ganzen Tag über probieren sie verschiedene Fahrgeschäfte aus, lachen und genießen Eis. Liams Lieblingsteil war die Zaubershow, bei der er auf die Bühne geholt wurde, um zu assistieren. „Das war super!", sagte er, immer noch aufgeregt.

Sie beendeten den Tag mit müden Lächeln, trugen Souvenirs und Erinnerungen an einen fantastischen Tag. „Können wir bald wiederkommen?", fragte Liam, bereits in Vorfreude auf ihren nächsten Besuch.

Vocabulary

Outing	Ausflug
Amusement park	Vergnügungspark
Roller coaster	Achterbahn
Ticket	Ticket
Fun	Spaß
Laugh	Lachen
Ice cream	Eis
Queue	Warteschlange
Ride	Fahrgeschäft
Souvenir	Souvenir
Map	Karte
Show	Show
Snack	Snack
Excited	Aufgeregt
Tired	Müde

Questions About the Story

1. *Where did Liam and his family spend their day?*

   a) At the beach
   b) In a museum
   c) At the amusement park

2. *What was Liam's reaction before the roller coaster ride?*

   a) Terrified
   b) Excited and nervous
   c) Bored

3. *What did Liam and his family do throughout the day?*

   a) Went hiking
   b) Visited different rides and enjoyed ice cream
   c) Played sports

4. *What was Liam's favorite part of the day?*

   a) Eating ice cream
   b) The roller coaster
   c) The magic show

5. *How did Liam participate in the magic show?*

   a) By watching
   b) By clapping
   c) By assisting on stage

Correct Answers:

1. c) At the amusement park
2. b) Excited and nervous
3. b) Visited different rides and enjoyed ice cream
4. c) The magic show
5. c) By assisting on stage

- Chapter Fifty-Eight -
THE NEW CLUB

Der neue Klub

Elena hörte von einem neuen Fotografieklub in der Schule und war begierig darauf, beizutreten. „Das könnte wirklich interessant werden", dachte sie und plante, zum ersten Treffen zu gehen.

Beim Treffen traf Elena andere Schüler, die ihr Interesse an der Fotografie teilten. Der Klubleiter diskutierte verschiedene Aktivitäten und Projekte, die sie durchführen könnten. „Ich habe so viele Ideen", teilte Elena aufgeregt mit der Gruppe.

Gemeinsam planten sie ihr erstes Event, einen Fotospaziergang am Wochenende im Park. „Es wird großartig sein, voneinander zu lernen", erkannte Elena und fühlte sich willkommen und inspiriert.

Teil des Fotografieklubs zu sein, half Elena nicht nur neue Freunde zu machen, sondern verbesserte auch ihre Fotografiefähigkeiten. Sie war froh, eine Gruppe gefunden zu haben, in der sie ihre Leidenschaft verfolgen und ihre Ideen einbringen konnte.

Vocabulary

Club	*Klub*
Member	*Mitglied*
Meeting	*Treffen*
Activity	*Aktivität*
Join	*Beitreten*
Interest	*Interesse*
Group	*Gruppe*
Weekly	*Wöchentlich*
Event	*Veranstaltung*
Organize	*Organisieren*
Leader	*Leiter*
Idea	*Idee*
Discuss	*Diskutieren*
Plan	*Planen*
Welcome	*Willkommen*

Questions About the Story

1. Why was Elena eager to join the new photography club at school?

    a) To meet the club leader
    b) To improve her photography skills
    c) Because she was interested in photography

2. What did Elena and the other club members plan as their first event?

    a) A photo exhibition
    b) A weekend photo walk in the park
    c) A photography competition

3. What was Elena's reaction to meeting other students at the photography club?

    a) She was intimidated
    b) She was excited and shared many ideas
    c) She decided to leave the club

4. How did joining the photography club benefit Elena?

    a) She became the club leader
    b) She made new friends and improved her photography skills
    c) She won a photography award

5. What was discussed in the first photography club meeting?

    a) The club's budget
    b) Club uniforms
    c) Various activities and projects

Correct Answers:

1. c) Because she was interested in photography
2. b) A weekend photo walk in the park
3. b) She was excited and shared many ideas
4. b) She made new friends and improved her photography skills
5. c) Various activities and projects

- Chapter Fifty-Nine -
THE COMMUNITY GARDEN

Der Gemeinschaftsgarten

In einer kleinen Stadt gab es einen wunderschönen Gemeinschaftsgarten, in dem jeder Gemüse und Blumen pflanzen konnte. An einem sonnigen Tag beschloss Sarah, im Garten freiwillig zu helfen.

„Zuerst werde ich einige Samen pflanzen", dachte Sarah, während sie in die Erde grub. Sie pflanzte Karotten und Tomaten und goss sie sanft. In der Nähe blühten bunte Blumen, die Schmetterlinge und Vögel anzogen und den Garten mit Leben füllten.

Mit der Zeit beobachtete Sarah, wie ihre Pflanzen wuchsen. Sie lernte Unkraut zu entfernen und Kompost zu verwenden, um den Boden reicher zu machen. „Schau dir all dieses Gemüse und diese Blumen an, die ich mitgeholfen habe zu züchten", sagte sie stolz.

Als die Erntezeit kam, sammelten Sarah und andere Freiwillige ihre Erträge. Sie hatten viele grüne Gemüse und schöne Blumen gezüchtet. „Dieser Garten bringt unsere Gemeinschaft zusammen", lächelte Sarah und fühlte sich mit der Natur und ihren Nachbarn verbunden.

Vocabulary

Garden	Garten
Plant	Pflanzen
Vegetable	Gemüse
Flower	Blume
Community	Gemeinschaft
Grow	Wachsen
Soil	Boden
Water	Gießen
Harvest	Ernten
Seed	Samen
Green	Grün
Nature	Natur
Volunteer	Freiwilliger
Compost	Kompost
Weed	Unkraut

Questions About the Story

1. *What did Sarah decide to volunteer for?*

    a) A community service project
    b) A local farm
    c) A community garden

2. *What type of seeds did Sarah plant?*

    a) Corn and peas
    b) Carrots and tomatoes
    c) Sunflowers and roses

3. *What attracted birds and butterflies to the garden?*

    a) The pond
    b) The colorful flowers
    c) The fruit trees

4. *What did Sarah learn to do in the garden?*

    a) Climb trees
    b) Remove weeds and use compost
    c) Make flower arrangements

5. *What was the result of Sarah and the volunteers' work?*

    a) The garden was closed
    b) They opened a new garden
    c) A lot of vegetables and flowers grew

Correct Answers:

1. c) A community garden
2. b) Carrots and tomatoes
3. b) The colorful flowers
4. b) Remove weeds and use compost
5. c) A lot of vegetables and flowers grew

- Chapter Sixty -
THE SCHOOL NEWSPAPER

Die Schülerzeitung

Tom war Redakteur der Schülerzeitung. Er war immer auf der Suche nach spannenden Nachrichten und Geschichten. „Diesen Monat werden wir Interviews mit unseren neuen Lehrern veröffentlichen", entschied Tom.

Er und sein Team arbeiteten hart daran, Artikel zu schreiben, Interviews zu führen und Fotos zu machen. „Wir müssen sicherstellen, dass alles vor der Deadline fertig ist", erinnerte Tom alle.

Am Tag der Veröffentlichung der Zeitung war Tom stolz. Schüler und Lehrer lasen ihre Arbeiten. „Dein Bericht über die Wissenschaftsmesse war wirklich interessant", sagte ihm ein Lehrer.

Teil des Zeitungsteams zu sein, lehrte Tom und seine Freunde die Bedeutung von Teamarbeit und Kommunikation. Sie waren froh, ihrer Schulgemeinschaft Nachrichten und Meinungen bieten zu können.

Vocabulary

Newspaper	Zeitung
Article	Artikel
Editor	Redakteur
Interview	Interview
Publish	Veröffentlichen
Report	Bericht
News	Nachrichten
Deadline	Deadline
Write	Schreiben
Column	Kolumne
Review	Rezension
Photograph	Fotografie
Issue	Ausgabe
Investigate	Ermitteln
Opinion	Meinung

Questions About the Story

1. *What role did Tom have in the school newspaper?*

    a) Writer
    b) Photographer
    c) Editor

2. *What did Tom's team plan to feature in the newspaper this month?*

    a) Sports events
    b) Interviews with new teachers
    c) Movie reviews

3. *What was Tom's reminder to his team about?*

    a) To interview more teachers
    b) To make sure everything is ready before the deadline
    c) To take more photographs

4. *How did Tom feel on the day the newspaper was published?*

    a) Disappointed
    b) Nervous
    c) Proud

5. *What feedback did Tom receive from a teacher?*

    a) The layout needed improvement
    b) The articles were too short
    c) The report on the science fair was interesting

Correct Answers:

1. c) Editor
2. b) Interviews with new teachers
3. b) To make sure everything is ready before the deadline
4. c) Proud
5. c) The report on the science fair was interesting

- Chapter Sixty-One -
THE TIME CAPSULE

Die Zeitkapsel

Frau Greens Klasse beschloss, eine Zeitkapsel zu erstellen. „Wir werden sie vergraben und in zehn Jahren öffnen", erklärte sie. Jeder Schüler schrieb einen Brief an sein zukünftiges Ich und legte einen kleinen Schatz dazu.

Sie fanden eine robuste Kiste und legten alles hinein. „Nun, lasst uns einen perfekten Ort finden, um unsere Zeitkapsel zu vergraben", sagte Frau Green. Sie wählten eine ruhige Ecke im Schulgarten.

Jahre vergingen, und der Tag, an dem die Zeitkapsel geöffnet werden sollte, kam endlich. Alle waren aufgeregt, ihre Briefe und Erinnerungen zu sehen. „Ich kann nicht glauben, wie viel sich verändert hat", sagte ein Schüler, während er seinen Brief las.

Die Zeitkapsel war eine Brücke zwischen Vergangenheit und Zukunft. Sie bewahrte ihre Geschichte und zeigte, wie sehr sie gewachsen waren. „Das war eine großartige Idee", stimmten alle zu, froh, ihre jüngeren Ichs wiederzusehen.

Vocabulary

Capsule	Kapsel
Time	Zeit
Bury	Begraben
Future	Zukunft
Letter	Brief
Memory	Erinnerung
Open	Öffnen
Past	Vergangenheit
Message	Nachricht
Discover	Entdecken
Year	Jahr
Treasure	Schatz
Box	Kiste
History	Geschichte
Preserve	Bewahren

Questions About the Story

1. *What did Mrs. Green's class decide to create?*

   a) A memory book
   b) A documentary film
   c) A time capsule

2. *What was the purpose of the time capsule?*

   a) To win a school competition
   b) To open it in ten years
   c) To hide from the school principal

3. *Where did the class choose to bury the time capsule?*

   a) In the school library
   b) In a quiet corner of the school garden
   c) Under the school's main hall

4. *What did each student add to the time capsule?*

   a) A picture
   b) A letter to their future self and a small treasure
   c) Homework assignments

5. *What did the students feel when they finally opened the time capsule?*

   a) Disappointment
   b) Excitement
   c) Indifference

Correct Answers:

1. c) A time capsule
2. b) To open it in ten years
3. b) In a quiet corner of the school garden
4. b) A letter to their future self and a small treasure
5. b) Excitement

- Chapter Sixty-Two -
A SURPRISE GUEST

Ein Überraschungsgast

Lucy veranstaltete eine kleine Party in ihrem Haus. Sie lud ihre Freunde und Familie ein, den Abend zu genießen. „Ich hoffe, jeder wird eine gute Zeit haben", dachte sie, während sie das Abendessen vorbereitete.

Plötzlich klingelte die Türklingel. „Wer könnte das sein?", fragte sich Lucy. Sie öffnete die Tür und fand einen Überraschungsgast: ihre Freundin Mia, die letztes Jahr ins Ausland gezogen war. „Mia! Was für eine wunderbare Überraschung!", rief Lucy aus und hieß sie herzlich willkommen.

Mia brachte Geschenke für alle mit, und ihre Ankunft machte die Party noch besonderer. Sie genossen alle das Abendessen, plauderten und lachten zusammen. Mia erzählte von ihren Abenteuern im Ausland, und alle hörten fasziniert zu.

„Es ist so schön, dich wiederzusehen", sagte Lucy. „Lass uns nicht wieder ein Jahr warten, um uns zu besuchen." Der Überraschungsgast machte den Abend für Lucy und ihre Gäste unvergesslich. Sie waren alle glücklich, zusammenzubleiben und die Gesellschaft des anderen zu genießen.

Vocabulary

Surprise	*Überraschung*
Guest	*Gast*
Welcome	*Willkommen*
Party	*Party*
Visit	*Besuch*
Friend	*Freund*
Dinner	*Abendessen*
Gift	*Geschenk*
Arrive	*Ankommen*
Happy	*Glücklich*
Chat	*Plaudern*
Invite	*Einladen*
Family	*Familie*
Stay	*Bleiben*
Enjoy	*Genießen*

Questions About the Story

1. *Who was having a small party at her house?*

    a) Mia
    b) Lucy
    c) Sarah

2. *What was Lucy's hope for the party?*

    a) That the food would be delicious
    b) That everyone would have a good time
    c) That the party would end early

3. *Who arrived at Lucy's house as a surprise guest?*

    a) A family member
    b) A neighbor
    c) Mia, her friend who had moved abroad

4. *What did Mia bring to the party?*

    a) A cake
    b) Gifts for everyone
    c) Flowers

5. *What was everyone's reaction to Mia's stories about her adventures abroad?*

    a) Bored
    b) Amazed
    c) Confused

Correct Answers:

1. b) Lucy
2. b) That everyone would have a good time
3. c) Mia, her friend who had moved abroad
4. b) Gifts for everyone
5. b) Amazed

- Chapter Sixty-Three -
THE ENVIRONMENTAL PROJECT

Das Umweltprojekt

Herr Smiths Klasse beschloss, ein Umweltprojekt zu starten. „Wir müssen unseren Planeten schützen", sagte er seinen Schülern. Sie stimmten alle zu, sich auf Recycling und das Säubern ihres lokalen Parks zu konzentrieren.

Die Schüler sammelten Abfall, trennten ihn zum Recycling und pflanzten neue Bäume. „Jedes bisschen hilft", erklärte Herr Smith, während sie zusammenarbeiteten, um aufzuräumen. Sie stellten auch Schilder auf, um andere dazu anzuregen, den Park sauber zu halten und zu recyceln.

Am Ende des Projekts sah der Park besser aus als je zuvor. Die Schüler waren stolz auf ihre Arbeit. „Wir haben wirklich einen Unterschied gemacht", sagten sie. Sie starteten eine Kampagne in ihrer Schule, um das Bewusstsein für die Wichtigkeit des Recyclings und der Energieeinsparung zu schärfen.

Ihr Projekt zeigte allen, dass sie durch Zusammenarbeit ihre Gemeinschaft grüner und sauberer machen konnten. Sie lernten, dass selbst kleine Handlungen große Auswirkungen auf die Umwelt haben können.

Vocabulary

Environment	*Umwelt*
Project	*Projekt*
Recycle	*Recyceln*
Clean	*Säubern*
Pollution	*Verschmutzung*
Plant	*Pflanzen*
Earth	*Erde*
Conservation	*Erhaltung*
Waste	*Abfall*
Green	*Grün*
Energy	*Energie*
Save	*Sparen*
Nature	*Natur*
Campaign	*Kampagne*
Awareness	*Bewusstsein*

Questions About the Story

1. *What was the main focus of Mr. Smith's class's environmental project?*

   a) Planting flowers
   b) Cleaning a local park and focusing on recycling
   c) Building birdhouses

2. *What did Mr. Smith tell his students about the importance of the project?*

   a) "We need to take care of our planet."
   b) "This is just for a grade."
   c) "It's too late to make a difference."

3. *What actions did the students take during their environmental project?*

   a) They only planted trees
   b) They gathered waste, separated it for recycling, and planted new trees
   c) They watched documentaries on recycling

4. *What did the students start in their school after the project?*

   a) A dance club
   b) A campaign to raise awareness about recycling and conserving energy
   c) A cooking class

Correct Answers:

1. b) Cleaning a local park and focusing on recycling
2. a) "We need to take care of our planet."
3. b) They gathered waste, separated it for recycling, and planted new trees
4. b) A campaign to raise awareness about recycling and conserving energy

- Chapter Sixty-Four -
A DAY AT THE AQUARIUM

Ein Tag im Aquarium

Anna und ihr Bruder Tom besuchten an einem sonnigen Samstag das Aquarium. „Ich kann es kaum erwarten, die Haie und Delfine zu sehen", sagte Tom aufgeregt, als sie eintraten.

Sie begannen ihre Tour am großen Becken, wo bunte Fische zwischen den Korallen schwammen. „Schau dir diesen riesigen Hai an!", zeigte Anna. Sie beobachteten staunend, wie der Hai durch das Wasser glitt.

Als Nächstes sahen sie eine Delfinshow. Die Delfine sprangen und machten Tricks, was alle zum Klatschen und Jubeln brachte. „Delfine sind so schlau", sagte Tom beeindruckt.

Sie lernten viel vom Guide, der ihnen über das Meeresleben erzählte und wie man das Meer und seine Kreaturen schützen kann. Anna und Tom sahen viele Ausstellungen, einschließlich einer mit im Dunkeln leuchtenden Quallen.

„Es war ein unglaublicher Tag", sagte Anna, als sie gingen. „Ich habe so viel gelernt und so viele schöne Fische gesehen." Sie versprachen, bald wiederzukommen, begierig darauf, mehr über die Unterwasserwelt zu erfahren.

Vocabulary

Aquarium	Aquarium
Fish	Fisch
Shark	Hai
Tank	Becken
Coral	Koralle
Marine	Meeres-
Dolphin	Delfin
Exhibit	Ausstellung
Sea	Meer
Tour	Tour
Water	Wasser
Creature	Kreatur
Guide	Führer
Learn	Lernen
Jellyfish	Qualle

Questions About the Story

1. *What activity did Anna and her brother Tom decide to do on a sunny Saturday?*

   a) Visit the zoo
   b) Go to the aquarium
   c) Attend a concert

2. *What were Tom's feelings about seeing sharks and dolphins at the aquarium?*

   a) Indifferent
   b) Scared
   c) Excited

3. *Which exhibit did Anna and Tom start their tour with at the aquarium?*

   a) Dolphin show
   b) Jellyfish exhibit
   c) Shark tank

4. *What did Tom find impressive at the aquarium?*

   a) The size of the sharks
   b) The intelligence of dolphins
   c) The color of the coral

5. *What did Anna and Tom do at sunrise at the aquarium?*

   a) Witnessed the canyon's illumination
   b) Took photographs
   c) Watched a dolphin show

Correct Answers:

1. b) Go to the aquarium
2. c) Excited
3. c) Shark tank
4. b) The intelligence of dolphins
5. a) Witnessed the canyon's illumination

- Chapter Sixty-Five -
THE COSTUME PARTY

Die Kostümparty

Emily war aufgeregt. Sie veranstaltete eine Kostümparty mit dem Thema Märchen. „Ich kann es kaum erwarten, alle Kostüme zu sehen", dachte sie, während sie ihr Haus mit bunten Lichtern und Masken schmückte.

Am Abend der Party kamen Freunde, verkleidet als verschiedene Märchenfiguren. Emily trug ein schönes Prinzessinnenkleid und ihr Freund Max kam als Ritter. Musik erfüllte den Raum, und sie tanzten und lachten gemeinsam.

Es gab einen Wettbewerb für das beste Kostüm. Alle stimmten ab, und Max gewann den Preis für sein kreatives Ritterkostüm. Sie spielten Spiele, aßen Snacks, und der Raum war erfüllt von Freude und Gelächter.

„Es ist die beste Party überhaupt!", waren sich alle einig. Die Kostümparty war ein Erfolg, und Emily war glücklich zu sehen, wie sehr ihre Freunde Spaß hatten.

Vocabulary

Costume	Kostüm
Party	Party
Dress up	Verkleiden
Theme	Thema
Mask	Maske
Dance	Tanzen
Music	Musik
Prize	Preis
Character	Figur
Fun	Spaß
Invite	Einladen
Decorate	Dekorieren
Snack	Snack
Game	Spiel
Laugh	Lachen

Questions About the Story

1. *What was the theme of Emily's costume party?*

    a) Pirate Adventure
    b) Fairy Tale
    c) Superheroes

2. *What costume did Emily wear to the party?*

    a) A pirate
    b) A fairy
    c) A princess

3. *Who won the best costume contest at the party?*

    a) Emily
    b) Max
    c) Sarah

4. *What did Max dress up as for the costume party?*

    a) A wizard
    b) A knight
    c) A dragon

5. *What activities did guests enjoy at the costume party?*

    a) Dancing and playing games
    b) Watching a movie
    c) Swimming

Correct Answers:

1. b) Fairy Tale
2. c) A princess
3. b) Max
4. b) A knight
5. a) Dancing and playing games

- Chapter Sixty-Six -
THE OLD MAP

Die alte Karte

Jack fand eine alte Karte auf dem Dachboden seines Großvaters. „Das sieht aus wie eine Schatzkarte", rief er aus. Die Karte führte zu einem verborgenen Schatz auf einer entfernten Insel, gekennzeichnet mit einem 'X'.

Voller Abenteuerlust nahm Jack seinen Kompass, die alte Karte und stach in See. Die Reise war voller Aufregung und Herausforderungen. Er navigierte durch raue See und erkundete unbekannte Pfade.

Den Hinweisen auf der Karte folgend, suchte Jack die Insel ab. Nach Stunden der Suche fand er das 'X' in der Nähe eines alten Baumes. Er grub und entdeckte eine Kiste voller Gold und Juwelen.

„Das ist das größte Abenteuer meines Lebens", sagte Jack, während er seinen Fund bewunderte. Die alte Karte hatte ihn zu einem echten Schatz geführt, genau wie in den Legenden.

Vocabulary

Map	Karte
Treasure	Schatz
Explore	Erkunden
Compass	Kompass
Adventure	Abenteuer
Island	Insel
X (marks the spot)	X (markiert die Stelle)
Search	Suchen
Find	Finden
Clue	Hinweis
Journey	Reise
Old	Alt
Legend	Legende
Path	Pfad
Discover	Entdecken

Questions About the Story

1. *Where did Jack find the old map?*

   a) In his grandfather's attic
   b) In a library book
   c) Buried in his backyard

2. *What did Jack believe the old map led to?*

   a) A hidden treasure
   b) A secret cave
   c) An ancient ruin

3. *Where was the treasure hidden according to the map?*

   a) Under a bridge
   b) Inside a cave
   c) On a distant island

4. *What did Jack use to navigate to the treasure?*

   a) A GPS device
   b) Stars
   c) A compass

5. *What challenge did Jack face on his journey?*

   a) Rough seas
   b) Desert crossing
   c) Mountain climbing

Correct Answers:

1. a) In his grandfather's attic
2. a) A hidden treasure
3. c) On a distant island
4. c) A compass
5. a) Rough seas

- Chapter Sixty-Seven -
A SPACE ADVENTURE

Ein Weltraumabenteuer

Lucy träumte davon, den Weltraum zu erkunden. Eines Tages wurde sie Astronautin und für eine Mission zum Mars ausgewählt. „Ich bin bereit für dieses Weltraumabenteuer", sagte sie, als sie die Rakete bestieg.

Als die Rakete startete, spürte Lucy den Nervenkitzel, die Erdanziehung zu verlassen. Sie sah Sterne, Planeten und die Weite der Galaxie durch die Fenster des Shuttles.

Die Mission umfasste die Umrundung des Mars, das Sammeln von Daten und die Suche nach Lebenszeichen. Lucy und ihr Team entdeckten einen seltsamen, leuchtenden Stein, der nicht vom Mars stammte. „Könnte er von Außerirdischen sein?", fragten sie sich.

Nach Abschluss ihrer Mission kehrten sie als Helden zur Erde zurück. Lucys Weltraumabenteuer war aufregender, als sie es sich jemals vorgestellt hatte, und machte sie begierig auf die nächste Reise unter den Sternen.

Vocabulary

Space	Weltraum
Rocket	Rakete
Planet	Planet
Star	Stern
Astronaut	Astronaut
Orbit	Umlaufbahn
Galaxy	Galaxie
Moon	Mond
Alien	Außerirdischer
Shuttle	Shuttle
Universe	Universum
Mission	Mission
Telescope	Teleskop
Launch	Start
Gravity	Schwerkraft

Questions About the Story

1. *What was Lucy's dream that came true?*

   a) Becoming a teacher
   b) Exploring the ocean
   c) Exploring space

2. *What planet was Lucy's mission focused on?*

   a) Mars
   b) Venus
   c) Jupiter

3. *What did Lucy and her team discover on their mission?*

   a) A strange, glowing rock
   b) A new form of life
   c) Water

4. *How did Lucy feel during the rocket launch?*

   a) Scared
   b) Thrilled
   c) Sick

5. *What was the purpose of Lucy's mission to Mars?*

   a) To plant a flag
   b) To orbit Mars and collect data
   c) To meet aliens

Correct Answers:

1. c) Exploring space
2. a) Mars
3. a) A strange, glowing rock
4. b) Thrilled
5. b) To orbit Mars and collect data

- Chapter Sixty-Eight -
THE LOST CITY

Die verlorene Stadt

Anna, eine Archäologin, war schon immer von der Legende einer in der Dschungel versteckten verlorenen Stadt fasziniert. Eines Tages fand sie in einem alten Buch eine antike Karte, die den Standort der Ruinen markierte. „Das könnte es sein", dachte sie, ihr Herz schlug vor Aufregung.

Mit ihrem Team machte sich Anna auf eine Expedition. Sie durchquerten den dichten Dschungel, geführt von der Karte. Nach tagelanger Suche stießen sie auf antike Ruinen, die von dicken Ranken bedeckt waren.

„Es ist die verlorene Stadt!", rief Anna aus. Sie erkundeten die Ruinen, fanden Artefakte und einen großen Tempel. Jede Entdeckung war ein Hinweis auf die Zivilisation, die einst dort blühte.

Als sie die Geheimnisse der Vergangenheit enthüllten, erkannte Anna, dass sie ein Rätsel gelöst hatten, das Archäologen seit Jahrhunderten beschäftigte. Die verlorene Stadt war nicht mehr nur eine Legende, sondern eine bemerkenswerte Entdeckung, die Licht auf eine antike Zivilisation warf.

Vocabulary

City	Stadt
Lost	Verloren
Ruins	Ruinen
Ancient	Antik
Explore	Erforschen
Mystery	Geheimnis
Expedition	Expedition
Map	Karte
Jungle	Dschungel
Discover	Entdecken
Artifact	Artefakt
Legend	Legende
Archaeologist	Archäologe
Temple	Tempel
Civilization	Zivilisation

Questions About the Story

1. *What inspired Anna to embark on her expedition?*

    a) A documentary
    b) A dream
    c) An ancient map

2. *Where was the lost city located?*

    a) In the desert
    b) Deep in the jungle
    c) Under the sea

3. *What did Anna and her team find in the ruins?*

    a) Gold coins
    b) A treasure chest
    c) Artifacts and a grand temple

4. *How did Anna feel when she first saw the ruins?*

    a) Terrified
    b) Excited
    c) Disappointed

5. *What did the expedition team use to guide them through the jungle?*

    a) The stars
    b) A compass
    c) An ancient map

Correct Answers:

1. c) An ancient map
2. b) Deep in the jungle
3. c) Artifacts and a grand temple
4. b) Excited
5. c) An ancient map

- Chapter Sixty-Nine -
THE MAGIC POTION

Der Zaubertrank

Elena, eine junge Hexe, war entschlossen, einen Zaubertrank zu brauen, der jede Krankheit heilen könnte. Sie hatte ein Rezept in einem alten Zauberbuch gefunden, benötigte jedoch seltene Zutaten. Das Rezept war ein Geheimnis, das über Generationen von Hexen weitergegeben wurde, ein Zeugnis für die Macht ihrer mystischen Kunst.

Mit ihrem Kessel bereit, machte sich Elena daran, die Zutaten aus dem verzauberten Wald zu sammeln. Sie fand magische Kräuter, verzaubertes Wasser und die seltene Mondblume, die nur bei Vollmond blühte. Diese Zutaten hatten die Kraft, die Gesundheit zu transformieren und Kranke zu heilen.

Zurück in ihrem Häuschen mischte Elena sorgfältig die Zutaten und sprach den Zauber. „Lass diesen Trank Heilung bringen", flüsterte sie, während der Trank brodelte und ein sanftes Leuchten ausstrahlte. Die Luft war erfüllt von einer mystischen Energie, als der Trank sich vor ihren Augen verwandelte.

Als sie schließlich den Zaubertrank abfüllte, wusste Elena, dass sie etwas Besonderes geschaffen hatte. Sie teilte ihn mit denen, die ihn benötigten, und der Trank wirkte Wunder, was ihr die Dankbarkeit vieler einbrachte. Das Geheimnis des Trankrezepts wurde zur Legende und inspirierte zukünftige Generationen.

Elenas Zaubertrank war ein Zeugnis für ihr Können und ihr Herz und bewies, dass man mit Entschlossenheit, einem Hauch Magie und den richtigen Zaubersprüchen die Welt verbessern konnte.

Vocabulary

Potion	*Trank*
Magic	*Magie*
Witch	*Hexe*
Spell	*Zauber*
Brew	*Brauen*
Cauldron	*Kessel*
Ingredient	*Zutat*
Enchant	*Verzaubern*
Bottle	*Abfüllen*
Secret	*Geheimnis*
Recipe	*Rezept*
Transform	*Verwandeln*
Power	*Macht*
Mystical	*Mystisch*
Heal	*Heilen*

Questions About the Story

1. *What was Elena determined to brew?*

   a) A love potion
   b) A magic potion to heal illnesses
   c) A potion for eternal youth

2. *Where did Elena find the recipe for the magic potion?*

   a) In an ancient spell book
   b) From a friend
   c) Online

3. *What was unique about the moonflower?*

   a) It glowed in the dark
   b) It was poisonous
   c) It only bloomed under a full moon

4. *What did Elena chant while mixing the potion?*

   a) A song of joy
   b) A traditional witch's hymn
   c) "Let this potion bring healing"

5. *What effect did the magic potion have?*

   a) It caused laughter
   b) It healed illnesses
   c) It turned things invisible

Correct Answers:

1. b) A magic potion to heal illnesses
2. a) In an ancient spell book
3. c) It only bloomed under a full moon
4. c) "Let this potion bring healing"
5. b) It healed illnesses

CONCLUSION

Congratulations on completing "69 Short German Stories for Beginners." You've embarked on a remarkable journey through the German language, guided by a collection of stories that transcend cultural and geographical boundaries, designed to universally appeal and engage your curiosity and imagination.

Your dedication to learning and expanding your German vocabulary through these tales reflects a commendable commitment to linguistic growth. These stories, carefully curated to cater to beginners, have provided you with a foundation in understanding and using German in a variety of contexts, equipping you with the skills necessary for everyday communication and beyond.

Embarking on the path of language learning is a journey of endless discovery, not just about the language itself but about the possibilities it unlocks. It is a bridge to new ways of thinking, a tool for connecting with others, and a means to explore the vast world of literature and communication.

I am eager to hear about your experiences and the adventures these stories have taken you on. Please share your journey with me on Instagram: **@adriangruszka**. Your progress, challenges, and insights are a source of inspiration and celebration. If this book has sparked joy in your language learning process, feel free to mention it on social media and tag me. Your feedback and stories are incredibly valuable.

For additional resources, deeper insights, and updates, visit **www.adriangee.com**. Here, you'll find a supportive community of fellow language learners and enthusiasts, as well as materials to further aid your exploration of the German language.

- Adrian Gee

CONTINUE YOUR LANGUAGE JOURNEY:
Discover "69 More German Stories for Intermediate Learners"

Are you on a quest to deepen your mastery of the German language and enrich your vocabulary even further? Have you surpassed the beginner stages and crave more complex narratives that challenge and delight? If you've nodded in agreement, then the next step in your linguistic adventure awaits!

"69 More German Short Stories for Intermediate Learners" is meticulously crafted for those who have already laid the groundwork with our beginner's collection and are ready to elevate their skills. This sequel not only broadens your linguistic horizons but also delves into more sophisticated themes and structures, perfectly suited for the intermediate learner eager for growth.

In this continuation of your German language journey, you will discover:

- A curated selection of engaging stories designed to fit the intermediate German learner's needs, ensuring a seamless transition to more advanced material.
- Enhanced vocabulary and grammatical structures, presented within compelling narratives that keep learning both effective and enjoyable.
- Cultural nuances and deeper insights into the German-speaking world, offering a richer understanding of the language's context and usage.
- Practical examples and exercises that reinforce your learning, encouraging active application and retention of new knowledge.

Don't let your language learning momentum fade. With "69 More Short German Stories for Intermediate Learners," you're not just advancing your German proficiency; you're immersing yourself in a world of captivating stories that inspire, educate, and entertain. Ready to take the next step in your German language journey and unlock new levels of fluency? Join us, and let's turn the page together towards intermediate mastery.

Made in the USA
Las Vegas, NV
17 June 2025

23759253R00256